Connections

Finding Your Place
in the
Natural World

Connections

DEBBY HAVAS

Connections

LITTLE POLLYWOG PRESS
JAY, NEW YORK

Editorial development and creative design support by Ascent:
www.spreadyourfire.net

Library of Congress Control Number: 2019909390
ISBN: 978-0-578-48919-3

Printed in the United States of America

for my grandsons,

Bladen Levi and Reid Russell,

may you always walk

with Nature

by your side

Contents

fall

winter

spring

summer

To My Readers

~~~~~~

You are about to embark on a journey into Nature, your own *personal* journey. Be prepared to encounter wonder, joy, beauty, peace, happiness, fun, and deep contentment.

Through these thirty-one brief excursions into the Natural World, I hope to introduce you to her wisdom in ways that will give you cause for reflection. Using Nature as a mirror, may you realize and apply aspects of that reflection to your own life.

You are invited to see what I am seeing and listen intently to the sounds I am hearing. Inhale deeply the subtle fragrances. Touch the world of Nature and feel her enter you, calming you with a peace-filled aura. Open your heart and allow Nature to touch your mind, encouraging you to interpret her message and incorporate her wisdom into your life.

Breathe in the scents carried on the wafting breeze. Reach out and touch what Nature offers freely to us. Let the feeling go deep, penetrating your very soul. Absorb her wisdom and consider the questions she invokes. Answer them as only *you* can do. Listen to her voices and let her wisdom touch you, giving you insights into your life.

What is Nature saying to you? What thoughts does she prompt within you? What feelings does she awaken within?

Are there stresses you need relief from; questions you seek answers to? Or do you just want to *be* for a while?

May your experience awaken new thoughts, ideas, and solutions. Perceptions you have had in the past may be broadened or changed completely. And may these written words guide you on *your* journey.

The path you are on. . . .

These inner excursions will lead you through the four seasons of the year, beginning with fall. I have always been enamored with fall; it is, for me, my favorite time of year. Fall speaks to me through the quieting down after the hectic pace of summer. Colors are brilliant and the scents—of fallen leaves, last of the flowers, first snow-scent in the wind—are both rich and unique. Temperatures are cooler. There is an anticipation of winter's stillness—a time for rest and recuperation.

As you travel through the seasons, you may wish to record your thoughts, reflections, and deeper understandings of things. Allow your heart and mind to be open to Nature's message for *you*. And may you discover the answers you seek, the peacefulness you desire.

And when you finish, may you truly have found and feel your *Connections, your* place in the Natural World. Then you will know you have found freedom—freedom in the present moment.

Fall, winter, spring, and summer—
how quickly time passes by.
Yet Nature's beauty is there to see
whenever we take the time.

fall

Waterfalls and turning leaves
beckon us to come—
And sit and be and feel her there
to calm us, relax us some.

winter

Water freezes, our breath we see—
icicles, snow, and cold.
We hunker down—it's wintertime;
"keep warm" is what we're told.

spring

Spring arouses everything—
sprouting and budding the gain.
Saps rise up, life renews;
and blossoms are kissed by rain.

summer

Summer speaks to us of warmth;
rainbows and sunsets are there.
Leaves and grasses are green again
and yet, are we aware

That Nature's gifts are there for us,
listen . . . watch . . . and see,
To accept the changes and live our lives—
Nature's model is the key.

Let Us Begin

M y canoe scrapes on the sandy shore as I ride the wake in with strong, forward strokes. Climbing out, my feet meet the sandy bottom as the water washes past my ankles—cool and inviting on my skin. I move to the bow of my boat and drag it up on the shore until it rests there securely. I reach over the gunnel and retrieve my hiking sneakers from the bottom of the canoe. Proceeding to the stern of the boat, I lean against the canoe while I rinse the wet, gritty sand off my feet and dry each in turn before placing them in my socks and sneakers. I firmly lace them up, and I'm ready to go.

I wonder what simple delight or adventure awaits me this time. I am standing in my beloved wilderness—an expanse of mountains, lakes, rivers, and ponds laced with paths that surrounds my home here in the Adirondack Mountains of upstate New York. More correctly, six million acres of wilderness and wonder.

I hesitate. Looking around, I take it all in—the lake, shore, sky, birds—and give thanks for the path that has led me to this point in my life. After a few moments, I reach down into the canoe and hoist my weathered backpack up and onto my shoulder. This backpack has been my constant companion on many a hike, kind of like an old, reliable friend. Inserting my arms, I secure the straps and take off into the woods.

The trail I found earlier in the week greets me and I begin to follow it, eager to see where it will lead me and what I will discover along the way. I love the intrigue and Nature's surprises. They are always there.

Will I find a feather cast off and lying at my feet, or see an unusual butterfly I'll need to identify? Will I find a moose track, large and emboldened in the mud, or view a wildflower the likes of which I've never seen before?

The path is well carved out and easy to follow. The lofty green ferns bordering it brush softly against my legs as I move along. Now and then a prickly branch intrudes upon my journey, poking into my skin and catching in my hair as I try to wrestle myself free. Eventually, the path seems to come to an end, and I stop. *What is it? What am I supposed to see here?*

I find myself in a mixed forest of beech, birch, and pine trees. Moss carpets the forest floor, and a flurry of ferns abounds. There are stumps of trees full of rot, hosting fungi perched as if on shelves, clinging to the dying stumps.

I see the old pines standing stalwart and strong as the sentinels of this forest, protecting all that dwell beneath.

The understory is filled with young trees and older saplings—birches and beeches—clustered near their parents. The bases of the trees house some grasses and wildflowers—trout lilies and painted trilliums—inconspicuous as any, yet looking staunch and full of purpose.

And I realize everything here has a purpose. The forest does not question that. There is a knowing—an inherent connection. The rain that falls and soaks into the moss which is protecting the soil is an example of that connection. The soil contains minerals that dissolve into the roots that grow the tree. The tree then drops its leaves, which nourish the soil and understory plants.

Anyone who loves gardening knows that carrots gain from being planted among tomatoes. It's a symbiotic relationship. Each uses what it needs from the soil, complementing the other's need to survive. Both benefit. The Native

Americans knew that corn, squash, and beans also have a symbiotic relationship. A sure way to improve the harvest is to plant them together.

Nature is truly wonderful.

I realize that this is a family—a gathering of plant "clans," if you will. This is *my* family. I am a member of all of this. The Natural World is my tribe.

I feel comforted by Nature, supported and filled with peace—even loved—when I am here. Here in the Natural World, Nature protects me and uplifts me. She magnifies my joy and lightens my grief. I feel accepted at whatever point I am in my life.

I have retreated into her great heart. I have come to her when I've been betrayed and have felt her absorb my pain. I have come to her with a heart fairly bursting and felt her magnify my intense joy. I have come to her when I seek an adventure, and she has willingly supplied a memorable experience, though maybe not what I was expecting.

I am calmed as I look up through the white pine branches, standing in awe at the beauty of their skyward reach. I marvel at the blending of all of Nature—the colors, the shapes, the sounds, the smells. The green shading of the branches against the blue hues of the sky brings tears to my eyes—tears of happiness as my soul fills with joy.

As my tears subside, I become aware of a persistent nuthatch beeping as it descends a tree trunk, looking for its dinner. I feel the warmth of the day as the hint of a breeze stirs my hair. I see myriad ants and spiders crawling over a fallen log.

I turn around and notice a dark rust-colored millipede making its way along the path behind me. *How do millipedes control all those legs?* I wonder. *Yet they do. They even seem to know where they are going. Do I?*

My worries take a back row to the vista spread before me as I welcome the Natural World into my life.

I feel a connection. I am an integral and necessary part of Nature. I belong. Here, I feel whole.

And I realize—I am one with Nature.

fall

Bumblebee, bumblebee,
Where have you gone?
I miss your flitting,
I miss your song.

No longer your buzzing
Do I hear
As you skitter to blossoms,
Far and near.

Come back to us, please
Come back again.
May you live among us,
May you call us "friend."

Barren Red Maple

~~~~~

Standing on my driveway, I find myself looking at the red maple tree that always turns a gorgeous red-orange in the fall. I'm barefoot, and the harsh gravel driveway challenges my tender feet. Yet I am totally distracted by the state of the red maple and hardly aware of any discomfort at all.

This year, the tree is quite different from every other fall I've witnessed—nineteen of them, to be exact.

A dry September caused the tree to begin to turn earlier than usual, the top turning red while the bottom branches remained green. The top leaves turned red one day, shriveled up a few days later, and then dropped from the tree a short time thereafter. Half the tree appeared barren, while the bottom leaves remained green.

A few weeks later, the rains came. Within days, the green bottom leaves began to turn the usual gorgeous red-orange and shone in all their glory for weeks afterward before being shed. The tree looked strange—barren at top and blossoming with vibrant color at the same time, as the tree's deep roots continued to feed the lower branches.

Nature was speaking loudly to me.

We all go through difficult times—times when we come close to giving up. How often have you said to yourself, "I just can't take any more of this"? We know we've reached our limit. We're at the end of it.

And then, we dig down . . . deep inside . . . and go on.

There is always a part of us, like the lower green branches, that is healthy and strong and vibrant. But that part becomes hidden by life's challenges—stress and grief and loss and just life itself, at times.

Nature shows us that our roots are as deep as those of the red maple, which live on to sprout again and again when properly watered. Leaves and even branches may die, but the roots will allow the tree to sprout again the following spring.

The red maple needed rain; what are *our* needs? What do we need to feel complete—to *be* complete? Is it surrounding ourselves with positive people, people who appreciate us? Is it feeling that we are accepted by someone just for being who we are, the real McCoy, so to speak? Is it being respected by our fellow workers? Is it performing our job to the best of our ability and having our employer take notice? Is it trying to see the positive in every situation life throws at us?

These are ways we can impart vitality to our body, in addition to fulfilling our basic needs. And each is as important as the other to allow us to feel complete—to *be* complete. Only then can we truly give of ourselves to our family, our job, and our community and use our own personal gifts to help others. And let's not forget our spiritual life—feeling we are a part of something greater than ourselves is the cohesion that holds all the parts together.

At times, we have all felt the lack in one or more of the areas mentioned above—being appreciated, being accepted for who we really are, having our work effort or talent noticed, being respected, having a positive outlook. How did we seek to fill the lack that we were experiencing? What did we try to substitute for that lack? Did we even recognize what it was that we were missing? Why did it happen? And what did we do about it? Did we do *anything* about it? Did we *learn* anything from our experience?

Isn't that what it's all about? Learning from our experiences? The red maple has deep roots, and so do we. We can sprout again. And we again can blossom with all our colors in vibrant array. What we need is a positive outlook and demeanor and to be open to *other* positives in our life. The more we focus on the positive, the more positives we will notice in our lives. Try it. It works.

Many years ago, I went through a divorce. It was a decision that took years of realization and careful thought. Enacting the decision and dealing with the resulting circumstances was one of my greatest challenges. I will never forget the day I left . . .

I approached my car with lingering footsteps, the dirt driveway feeling firm and solid beneath my feet. This was it.

Placing my hand on the door handle, I hesitated. Looking at my blue Ford Escort that I had purchased myself, I wondered, *Did I have to do this? Really do this?* I pushed the button, rotating the handle inward. The door began to open. As it did so, I felt an opening up within me, also. *But an opening of what? To what?* The answer came: *an opening to my future.*

This is it. It will never be the same, I thought. I looked around at my gardens with blossoms dancing in the breeze. The trees surrounding my house stood so vibrant and alive, gently swaying, caressed by the summer winds. This had been my home for the past twenty-one years. Here I had laughed and cried, hoped and dreamed. Here I had raised my two daughters with all the love I could muster. And here I had decided what I had known for quite some time—I had to go. I had to leave. I had to live apart from *him*.

But it wasn't supposed to be like this, I cried in silent agony. *I wasn't supposed to live apart from my girls.*

That inkling of a thought had never entered my mind.

I had used a great deal of time and energy over the years trying to save a dying marriage. But nothing I tried had worked. I even tried changing myself, to no avail. Yet some of my demons hunkered nearby, and my husband hadn't even begun to identify his at this time. So, here I was, opening my car door. Here I was—saying goodbye.

Standing there, the doubts began to bombard me. I felt like I was being pelted by wind-driven sand, biting and sting-ing. *Is this the best action for me to take right now? How will my girls be? My Mom didn't leave her marriage no matter how hard it got. Am I being selfish, knowing I have to go and acting on that feeling?* I stood there, gazing into my car, my mind racing, time crawling by.

The interior of my car seemed warm and welcoming, beckoning me to enter. Sitting there, hands resting in my lap, I slowly became aware of a further opening within me as if someone or something had unlocked the door to my heart, my soul. I took a deep breath; I could finally breathe.

I waited a few moments, breathing deeply and allowing the sense of freedom to take up residence within me. I straightened my torso and placed both hands on the steering wheel. Then I turned the key in the ignition and the engine sparked. I could feel my car come alive—vibrant with its own energy.

Slowly, carefully, I pressed the accelerator, giving impetus to the car. It was as though I was transferring my energies to it, and it was absorbing and integrating them into its own system. We were bonded. I felt a real sense of connection with my vehicle, like we were in this together—bosom buddies in our venture—creeping up the 400-foot driveway to who knew where?

Just as quickly, the pain began—heart-wrenching pain. As I gave force to the gas pedal, my eyes also gave force, and tears erupted. I could feel my heart tearing and ripping on its torturous journey as it divided itself in two. One part remained with my girls at the house. The other part I was taking with me.

Would the two parts ever mend themselves? I had to believe that could happen one day, *would* happen one day. This divide was the best for all of us, including my husband.

I had always been farsighted. We could and *would* all grow and gain from this action I was taking. But, as with all growth, there would be pain involved—much pain.

Right now, my pain seemed nearly impossible to endure. It tore me apart, thinking my girls might feel that I had abandoned them.

That was my greatest fear.

I felt like I was the frog we dissected in a college lab experiment, peeling back the skin, layer by layer, to expose the muscle structure and then peeling away muscle to expose the skeleton. That's how I felt—bare bones.

Only my faith was still intact, faith that I was doing what had to be done. This had to happen for all four of us to come out of this in a better, happier state.

The house meant little to me. It was a material object. My girls, however, meant everything.

I brought the car to a halt at the top of the small hill at the end of our driveway. I could feel the tears as they cascaded down my face. Turning my head, I looked down the road. I turned the wheel to the left as I pressed the accelerator and continued onto the road—the road that would lead to the rest of my life . . .

Sometimes we just know what we're supposed to do, even without understanding it all. And we accept the challenge without knowing what the results will be. That's where trust and faith come in. That's where we can stand strong and colorful even though our circumstances have diminished.

I experienced self-doubt at times, and lessened self-confidence. Financial issues were always present as I sought to find a full-time job with which to support myself. There was house maintenance to deal with and holiday plans, all of this by myself.

And then there were the lonely times . . .

I found my solace in Nature. She helped restore my self-confidence and belief in the future. She has always been there for me—always willing to share her wisdom and constancy. My continuing challenge is to remain open and willing to read her message.

Are you open and willing? Remember the barren maple. By focusing on the positives around us, we will not only feel better deep inside, but we'll be able to meet life's challenges with a more positive outlook and be happier people—not barren at all, but bursting with an array of color.

The Seed

~~~~~

Have you ever watched a seed go floating by airborne? What are you thinking as you watch it pass? What are you *feeling* in those fleeting moments as you watch it drift by? I begin to recall. . . .

It's 8 o'clock in the morning. I'm standing at my kitchen sink, finishing the breakfast dishes. As I give the last cereal bowl a final swish with the dish cloth, I lift my eyes and glance out the window. I enjoy viewing my small flower garden, situated about ten feet away from the house, and especially the lone milkweed plant that had begun to grow during late spring. After it sprouted, I watched it grow, inch by inch. It grew and blossomed with the sweetest-smelling flowers of anything in my garden. And did the bees and butterflies adore that plant!

It has now reached a height of five feet. The flowers have been replaced by green pods that I know contain a multitude of seeds.

Movement catches my eye, and my gaze settles on one pod in particular that had split open slightly, exposing the delicate seeds within. As I watch, a slight breeze stirs the open pod and one lone seed takes to the air. With its soft, white, fluffy parachute intact, it rises and then gently glides past the window. Momentarily, it gets hung up on the seeded spike of a brilliant pink-purple liatris flower. Then a gust dislodges it and carries it farther—up and over—and lands it on the ground.

I wonder if it will stay there or again be uplifted and moved to a better place. And will this be repeated over and over again until the seed is finally securely settled where it can sprout and grow?

If it lands on water, it cannot survive, though it requires water to grow. If it lands on a leaf or a tree limb, it cannot survive, for it needs a source of nutrition—a place to grow roots. But if it lands on fertile soil, it has an anchor and a place to begin.

Where did *you* land many years ago? And where are you now?

It is often a good investment of our time to reflect on our past, not to dwell on its positive or negative aspects, but simply to reflect on all that we have gone through during life's journey. I, for one, was not planted on pristine soil economically or materially, emotionally or psychologically. But I had a dream, and it developed and grew and modified over time.

We don't have to have pristine conditions, but we do need a deep desire—soul deep—even if we forget about it for a while. It can grow in silence without our focus at all. Life's circumstances and the choices we make sometimes interfere with that dream.

But why do we have that specific dream? Isn't it because we actually have the *ability* to bring it to fulfillment? Or maybe an adaptation of it?

When I was growing up, there was an old player piano in the house that my older sister took lessons on for eight years. I wanted to play the clarinet; I loved its haunting sound. I was told I had to take piano lessons or none at all. My family didn't have the money to rent the additional instrument. So I tried taking one year of piano lessons and that was it;

I really wanted to play the clarinet. The clarinet lessons never happened. As an adult, I came to understand the economics of it all.

I later took that disappointment and made sure that if my own children showed any interest in playing an instrument, I would find the money for them to pursue their interest in playing *whatever* instrument they chose.

Now, at age seventy, I could still fulfill my dream of playing the clarinet if I wanted, modifying my expectations of great success at it. But now I choose to spend my time and energy with other interests. Every now and then, though, I catch myself humming the clarinet solo "Stranger on the Shore," which I listened to hundreds of times on my brother's record player while growing up.

There are always choices in this life for us, even if we decide *not* to choose. Are you like the milkweed seed that gets tossed about by the wind, taking the chance it will make it to fertile ground? Or do you *choose* to make the best of wherever you are?

I look outside my window
As a seed goes flying by,
Encapsulated in puffy white
And gliding through the sky,

As if on wings—it sails so free,
On its own journey, yet to be.

Will it come to rest on root or limb,
On sand or water puddled thin?

With ne'er a care, I watch it fly
Till it disappears up in the sky.

And where it lands—will it take root
And bud and blossom, with seeds to boot?

Or will it lie there, dry and still
With no motivation to get up and will

Itself to grow and burst into bloom,
Remaining stagnant in its stone cold tomb?

At times, we seem to float through life, like seeds drifting on the wind. And I wonder what my life would have been like if I'd *chosen* a different path—moved to a different town, married a different mate, selected a different job. . . .

But I didn't and this is where my life is now. What about the future? Where will I land next? And will I grow there or choose to die?

At times we stagnate, but wherever life or the choices we make lead us, we can always get up and grow and burst into bloom, *if we so choose.*

~~~~~~~~

Where are *you* now?

Where would you like to *go*?

Red Squirrel

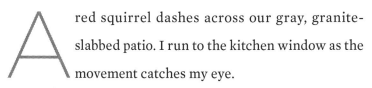

A red squirrel dashes across our gray, granite-slabbed patio. I run to the kitchen window as the movement catches my eye.

In its mouth, I can see a pine cone it has picked up from the ground beneath our white pines on the knoll. The cone is newly dropped—tight, green, and filled, no doubt, with plenty of fresh, nutritious seeds. Ripe for storing for the coming cold, dark months of winter. And I wonder. . . .

Am I prepared?

The dim, dark days of winter lie on the horizon like a blanket, promising to descend on us, leaving us with fewer hours of daylight. And what about the cold? Will we be treated to twenty degrees below zero, as we sometimes are?

Nature reminds me to stock up like the squirrel. No time like the present to begin my list in case I can't get out at some point this winter. Snowy, icy roads can get nasty to travel on, and the older I get, the less I look forward to driving on them. I may even get snowed in, as has happened in the past. And the power may go out.

All good reasons to be prepared. The squirrel has delivered a message I heed, and I take inventory.

What do I need in order to feel prepared for winter's challenges? A flashlight and extra batteries and extra warm clothes would be important. Extra food—canned and jarred—and dried seeds, nuts, grains, beans, and pastas, which store easily and long-term. A collection of paper products would come in handy, too.

Keeping warm could be an issue during the winter months, as could keeping frozen food cold. I need to think about storing water for drinking and flushing the toilet, etc. And what would we use for lights without electricity?

I best spend some time actually developing a plan.

I'm sure I'll think of other things, but this is a start: food, fuel, lights, water. We'll be okay. Thank you, red squirrel, for reminding me. . . .

A different thought comes to mind. There seems to be

something else in the message, "Be prepared," and I let my mind go in a completely different direction.

The opposite of be prepared is . . . be *spontaneous*. How do I feel about that?

I've never been comfortable with spontaneity, but I have gotten more comfortable with it over time, and I feel I'm healthier for it. I begin to think about the advantages and disadvantages of being prepared *versus* being spontaneous.

Having a plan gives me a sense of security, which was quite lacking in my growing up years, as I explained in my first book, *My Journey to Wholeness*. It makes me feel calm and relaxed. I can always adapt to a *change in my plan*, which most certainly is going to happen. Still, I am more comfortable having one.

Having a plan denotes a quality of certainty, which I like. But having a plan can sometimes give the planner a false sense of being able not only to direct the outcome but control it. And that is not possible.

In my earlier days, adjusting to a change in my plan could really throw me into a very confused state. My whole personality would become different. I would withdraw and become uncommunicative. I couldn't laugh or even smile. My heart would feel as if it had sunken to the depths. It would take hours for me to rise out of it enough to function on an even keel again.

It's still a challenge for me to plan and yet remain realistic about the *possible* other outcomes and to stop myself from over-focusing on the *ideal* outcome. If I fail to keep other possibilities in view, I create a lot of stress for myself.

In praise of planning: A plan allows for a specific focus. An organization of thoughts is required, which can transcend into a smoother-running outcome even if a change has taken place. People without a plan may appear *scattered* as they jump from one thing to another, never completing anything. That's another advantage—planning assumes a goal has been set and closure will be achieved.

In contrast, spontaneity allows me the freedom to choose on the spot; it's an adventure into the unknown. It requires me to trust in the Universe for on-the-spot guidance with little forethought of what result my words or actions may have. That can have a positive effect on me. It can allow me to be stress-free for a period of time. My mind begins to wander back. . . .

When Gary and I retired from teaching, we decided to take a trip to Maine. We only knew of two things we wanted to do on our trip—visit the L. L. Bean store and see the ocean. We consulted a map to see the most direct route to follow from the Adirondack Mountains in New York to Freeport, Maine, where L. L. Bean was located at the time. We wanted to avoid main roads if possible, agreeing that experiencing the countryside was the most important factor to us.

We had no idea how long it would take us to get to Freeport, so we didn't make reservations anywhere. We decided we'd stay wherever we ended up at the end of the day. We packed some clothes, a lunch, some snacks, and water and took off.

At first the excitement of the trip took over. As the hours passed, however, I became anxious, wondering if we'd find a place to stay. I chased my fears away by noticing the beauty of the countryside we were passing through. The more I concentrated on it, the more beauty I seemed to see.

Then we came across a sign directing us to a short trail to the top of a small mountain. And since we both loved to climb mountains, we instantly agreed to park the car and go. It was fun! I felt like an explorer seeking a way into the forest without any knowledge of where I was going or what I would see. And the view was great!

We ate our snack at the summit, then followed the trail back to the car and took off again. Hours later, we saw another sign at Crawford Notch, New Hampshire. We readily decided to turn off the route we were on and take the opportunity to drive to a look-out. What a spectacular view! We were looking at the White Mountain National Forest. We learned the names of many mountains new to both of us and were certainly glad we had taken the side-trip.

We didn't know how far we'd get that day, and again I was a little unnerved by that fact. How surprised we were in the late afternoon when we checked the map and saw we were close to Freeport. That's where we'd spend the night, after all. I began calling for a room and got one on my third try. It was a wonderful motel that had just opened a new wing, which made available rooms plentiful.

We went to L. L. Bean the following day and spent time walking a small, quiet beach on a bay near our motel, drifting along, watching the sun set on the water. I must say I was getting used to the slow, unscheduled pace. I felt a deep sense of calm overtake my whole being.

Sitting there on the sand as the skies put on their dance of colors left me feeling whole and peace-filled. No schedule ever exuded that same sense. And I was glad. I felt truly free and relaxed and became aware of how extremely healing and necessary it was for me to experience unplanned time.

The following day we inquired as to a larger beach where we could see and hear the sound of ocean waves. We were directed to an area some miles up the road.

The day was colder and windy; it was mid-September in Maine. We bundled up and sat on the beach, listening to the rhythm of the waves as they hypnotized us with their consistent cadence. It was the widest beach I had ever seen, never having spent time at the ocean before.

Not thinking about the tide, we decided to walk farther out on the sand to a mound of flat, gray rocks clustered there. We stood for a while, feeling the spray from the waves as they impacted against the irregular mass.

All of a sudden I became aware of the intensity of the waves. The spray shot higher and harder. The sound of the waves had a quality of harshness to it and was a great deal louder. I turned around to see the beach and was horrified that there was water separating us from where we'd been sitting previously. The beach had shrunk! The tide was coming in!

We jumped off the rocks and raced back to our towels with water lapping at our knees. My fear was real.

We hurriedly gathered everything up and retreated to the rear of the beach as my heart pounded. From there we watched the water reclaim the entire area.

I gained a deep appreciation for the tides that day. I was amazed at how quickly and forcefully the landscape had changed and how innocently people can become endangered. A need for *some* planning, indeed.

Looking back on our three days of experiencing spontaneity, I found it to be a wonderfully relaxing and freeing time. I felt calm and patient. I knew I could handle any stress that might arise.

My experience convinced me that we need a balance of both being prepared *and* living our lives spontaneously to maintain a semblance of health.

Since I am more comfortable with being organized and having a plan, I find myself, at times, *craving* spontaneity. When I feel myself becoming too regimented in my thinking or doing, I *need* to just go somewhere—*unplanned*—come what may. It just feels right. It feels *good*. I'm trying to incorporate more spontaneity into my life. I know I need to do that to keep me more balanced.

Sometimes our profession requires us to be more prepared and organized. Consequently, we may find ourselves already needing to function more spontaneously in our personal life.

~~~~~

Which are you more comfortable with: being prepared or being spontaneous? Are there ways you can incorporate more of the one you experience less often?

In contrast to our human experience, Nature tries to show us how to keep in balance. Create balance in your own life and watch the healthy changes that emerge.

Fall at Buttermilk Falls

~~~~~~

t's a clear day as I head to Buttermilk Falls, a gorgeous cascade on the river near where I used to live in Long Lake, New York. I ease my car to the side of a small pull-off area and roll to a stop. I see a trail sign as I look out at the hardwood forest, pointing my way to the falls. My excitement begins to mount. Leaving my car behind, I take to the woods.

The scent of fall greets me—a combination of dry and decaying leaves. Here in the Adirondack Mountains the maple trees have begun their shutting down, ceasing their normal production of chlorophyll. Without the green of the chlorophyll, their other vibrant colors show through. There are yellows, oranges, and reds with myriad hues of each—pure beauty.

I walk along the short path that's been worn bare by the many who have visited before me. Colorful leaves are filtering down from above. A slight breeze catches them, increasing their momentum as they drift toward the ground, striking twigs and branches along the way. The sound of this reminds me of a light rain falling—so much so that I automatically begin to lift the hood on my jacket before catching myself, realizing the source of the sound; all around me the trees are shedding their multicolored leaves as an offering in preparation for winter.

Aside from the dropping leaves, I begin to recognize another sound—that of the falls. With piqued awareness, I hurry on.

As I get closer, I see gray granite boulders strewn about. They seem to stand as if in protection of the falls, guarding the flow of water and funneling the mounting roar I hear.

The force of the water seems to elicit a certain fear within me—a caution, at the very least. The falls speak loudly to me of the power I am witnessing as the water pounds the rocks, wearing them smooth.

I move closer and feel the spray as it lands on my skin—a tickling sensation, yet the coolness of it is quite refreshing, awakening an alertness within me. I begin to see the beauty of it all.

As the sun reflects upon the frothy white foam, a kaleidoscope of color appears. Rainbows of water droplets arise where the sun's rays illuminate the spray as it is forced upward by the water striking the boulders. Over and over, I watch the effect.

My awareness again moves to the sound of the water flowing over the boulders. I am struck by the constancy and consistency of it. And I am made aware that life has a constancy all its own. Situations and choices cause *changes* to occur but it—*life*—remains.

As I look at the waterfall, I notice an amazingly calm area right below it. The water seems at peace there, slowly fanning outward like the spokes of a wheel.

I think of how we go through such traumatic times in our lives and yet we emerge a little calmer. Eventually, we may even find the peace we are seeking.

I remember being diagnosed with Multiple Sclerosis when I was thirty-seven years old. I have described the initial trauma and the detailed aftermath in my memoir, *My Journey to Wholeness.* The peace I sought came about gradually over many years of doubting and struggle. But it came.

The peace came.

It doesn't have to take being diagnosed with a chronic illness to qualify as a traumatic experience. It can be the loss of a job, a loved one, a dear friend, a relationship. It can be the loss of a pet or an ability or our dignity or a tradition. Even an embarrassing situation or comment can be traumatic for a person.

Then there are those who are traumatized by aging into the elder years. Some people age gracefully, adapting as they go, while others resist the changes.

Trauma involves loss. It is specific to the individual involved. We each experience loss in a different way. We can sympathize; we can empathize. But we cannot know the depth of the loss for another person. The *cause* of the loss is secondary. Whatever we lost is gone, and it's *never* coming back. And even if we could get the loss back, it wouldn't be the same as the first time around.

My eyes are drawn to the trees bordering the falls, and I watch as they drop their leaves into the turmoil below. They are thrust about, being pulled under and then rising again only to float downstream to who knows where.

In life, *I* have felt thrust about, and it seemed as if *I* were being pulled under and almost drowned. I have felt overwhelmed by life's events—loss . . . grief. . . . Yet I rose to the surface where I could breathe again. Maybe not as fully or as deeply as before, but with *new* breath and with *new* life.

As a result, I began to see things differently. My perception of people and of situations changed.

Life and change are synonymous. Change *in* life remains a constant. We can be assured of that.

I have changed, becoming more open, more sensitive, more accepting, more compassionate and more loving than I was in my earlier life.

The falls speak loudly to me of journey and illusion, for we do not know what tomorrow will bring. We have only today to live and await the change life guarantees us. Like the leaves that bring forth the hidden colors. Like the gifts we unknowingly share just by being ourselves. Like the gifts we carry within that blossom forth when given the opportunity.

We are like the water that flows over the falls, not really knowing where our journey will lead us, but remembering and yearning for the calm and peaceful times in our life after struggle and turmoil.

Think of a particular struggle you've come through. What have you learned? Are you now at peace?

Are you *presently* struggling in an area of your life? Take a walk in Nature and bring this challenge to mind. Tell her about it; speak it out loud. Then listen, watch, observe. Open yourself up to her insights. Let your heart hear her message.

5

Scarred White Ash

~~~

The clear sky fairly glistens with a deep, rich shade of blue today. The light flickers through the trees as I walk briskly down the forest path near my home. I inhale deeply, breathing in the familiar scent of pine.

Being outside always energizes me. Breathing deeply of Nature's many scents enlivens my spirit, replacing my emptiness with a feeling of wholeness.

A few chickadees bounce from limb to limb, moving along. They serenade me with their familiar chirp—*chick-a-dee-dee-dee.*

The path finally turns and I round the corner. I am shaded by hemlock and balsam growing here, interlocking their branches overhead like arms in an embrace. It makes me feel as if I'm in a tunnel of green, and I love it. Continuing on, what looks like an old, dead tree trunk comes into view.

I'm always amazed at how I can walk down the same path, over and over, day after day, and yet my experience is still different—like today.

I've passed this dead tree trunk every time I've jaunted down this path and never stopped and really *seen* it until today. Today it's calling to me, calling to me to come closer and take notice.

As I near the trunk, I notice that the scar I've so often seen races up from the ground level vertically about fifteen feet. Wider at the bottom, it gradually decreases to its apex. I'd always assumed the tree had been struck by lightning and had died. But as I stand there, looking at the uppermost point of the scar, I realize it isn't dead at all.

It had obviously been damaged years ago. Sap was no longer flowing, nor did I see any traces of sap that had long ago dried up. The outer bark had been split open and the inner bark was exposed. The passage of time was having its effect, causing the bark to take on a gray smoothness that beckoned me to reach out and touch it. And so I did, connecting with the crippling event of long ago. This tree had struggled for years to overcome its trauma. It had kept on going and growing even though it was maimed.

I tilt my head back and let my gaze follow the scar skyward. Then something green catches my eye toward the top. *What is that?* Then I can see another swatch of green and another . . . and another. . . . Leaves.

The ash tree is still *alive*.

Even though it was scarred years before, it has continued to *grow* and *adapt* and *live*.

Isn't that what we do when adversity comes our way? And I begin to become aware of the strength it took for this tree to overcome its trauma and keep on going.

We, too, need strength to overcome our scars and keep on going, maybe even growing a bit stronger as a result.

I am in awe. This tree was able to grow taller and continue producing leaves and seeds, adapting to the lasting effects of its trauma.

I think about how anything can happen to us in life. We might become physically crippled by an accident. Part of our body may not regain its function as well as before the accident. Yet a person can still grow and learn and become a contributing member of society, in most cases. We can become stronger as we train other body parts to overcome or compensate for what we see as a deficit.

A chronic illness may also cause us to feel scarred as we struggle to adapt to our limitations. When I was diagnosed with Multiple Sclerosis, I realized I had to give up one of my favorite activities—mountain climbing. And I *loved* climbing mountains.

My fatigue was paramount, and I could never count on the amount of energy I would have on any given day. With fatigue there's no pushing yourself to go a little farther or to do a little more. There just isn't. I would be overcome by a wash of fatigue and that would end my activity. I had to lay my body right down, then and there. That was the only thing that would relieve it. At first, I needed to rest for a couple of hours. Gradually the length of time lessened. Most of the time, I didn't even go to sleep; I just had to make myself prone. Up until that time, I never knew fatigue could be so crippling.

Then there are the emotions such as anger, fear, envy, jealousy, and bitterness that can become crippling, be it in attitude or behavior. If we're usually negative about things, people will begin to distance from us. Don't *we* feel better being around someone who has a positive outlook? Don't we feel lifted up by them?

Disagreeing with a positive person is a whole different experience from disagreeing with a negative person. With a positive person, I am usually able to see where they are coming from and even gain some insights. I am calm and listening. We part as friends. With a negative person, I feel challenged, and that I need to fight for my viewpoint. There is a clamp on my heart, and I withdraw within to protect myself from their tone. I experience the anxiety for a long time afterward.

I once worked with a teacher who constantly complained about her students during lunch break. I had the misfortune of having the same break time. The room we ate in had only the one table, and so I had to listen to her negativity day in and day out. I began to feel badly for her students, because they could never attain worthiness of her praise. They were all in that "no win" atmosphere, even the ones who were accomplishing something. After many attempts at gearing the conversation to a more positive route and failing to do so, I began eating my lunch in my classroom.

A person who has a negative take on everything really drains me. I tire of all the negativity, and it brings me down. People who are consistently negative are unhappy people, and it rubs off on others. I find I feel uplifted being around a positive person, even if I disagree with the opinion expressed.

Anger can leave deep scars for the one expressing it and for the one on the receiving end. I shy away from angry people. I find they usually refuse to see another side to their dilemma. People can be hurt by the way the anger is expressed. Physical or psychological abuse may result. Repetitive instances of humiliation or manipulation may also come about as the sense of power and control enters in—one person over another.

And then there is fear. I once had a fear of snakes. Growing up, I often witnessed my mother smashing them with a rock whenever she saw one. They were the "devil."

When I first bought my house, I had a frightening experience. The rough-cut pine siding played host to a snake inching its way up toward the window. I was engulfed in fear when I saw that and raced inside, closing all windows and doors. Being alone, I sat down with my heart racing. I felt as if my safety was being invaded.

After a few minutes, my curiosity got the best of me, and I wondered where the snake had gotten to. I crept outside to where I had seen it before. It was still there, but now it was stretched out, all four feet of it! I sat down and became amazed not only by watching it carefully begin to move but also by the beauty of the pattern of colors on its scales. Minutes passed. Finally, it carefully made its way down to the ground and slithered into the garden. When I went back inside, I checked out my book on reptiles, identifying my snake as a milk snake and learning about its habits and diet. I could feel the fear melting away.

I saw the snake many times after that and for many years, but it never scared me again. I came to look upon the snake as my friend, waiting for it to arrive late spring, greeting it when I went outside. Sometimes I would see it sunning itself or lying curled up and sleeping. I never again saw it climbing on the side of my house. I had conquered my fear; I was stronger because of my experience.

Nature had reminded me again of how we may be scarred by life's circumstances, but we can go on, having gained in strength. We can still have a quality of life by adjusting to and overcoming our potentially crippling state. We can sprout green leaves like the ash tree and even produce seeds. Carrying our scar will help many others to accept *their* scars and become stronger.

Have you become scarred in some way, physically, emotionally, or psychologically? Are you still crippled by your scar, or has it made you stronger? How can it strengthen you?

Morning at My Pond

~~~~~

My spring-fed pool is in shadow as I approach, the soft sphagnum mosses guiding my feet. It is morning. The air is still; not a leaf is stirring. My pool doesn't even match the length or width of a regulation swimming pool, but it's mine. I call it my pond, and it's my favorite place to be.

The smell of autumn is in the air—the scent rising from dried fallen leaves that cover the path. But this year it's different. There's little color in them. It's been a dry September—the leaves are drying and dropping before they turn their vibrant colors.

I feel a pang of sadness, remembering how I would search for just the right blend of hues and thrill at my find.

Just then a lone, colored leaf, having escaped the effects of the dryness, drifts down in front of me. I stop and gently lift it, admiring the unusual swim of color. Then I return it to its resting place to continue its journey of decay, becoming food for next year's growth.

As I near the pond, I see the water level has dropped a foot and a half. The shallow end has no water at all. That's where the frogs lay a multitude of eggs in the spring, their jellied masses floating on the surface. That's also where the outlet is located. When the pond is high, a trickle of water weaves its way to a small holding bowl below.

Sitting down on the wooden boardwalk above the water, I look around and listen. There's a kind of insect that chirps constantly in the fall, filling the air with continual background sound. Noticing the sound reminds me that I'll have to go on an identity search when I get back to the house. I know the sound is neither the peepers of spring nor the crickets of fall. But what is it?

I remove my shoes and socks and dip my toes into the water—cold at 51 to 54 degrees F. The temperature doesn't waver much no matter how warm the days become.

The pond is fed by a spring beneath a sunken rock in the pond. It's the perfect temperature for salamanders and pollywogs to grow and complete metamorphosis, but a little hard for me to get used to. I rarely submerge my entire body. I splash some water on myself and continue soaking my feet to cool off.

Now and then a frog jumps in the water. I can hear the characteristic *thump-drip* of its splash.

I can see that the pollywogs have grown their legs. Soon their tails will begin to gradually disappear, becoming shorter and shorter as they prepare for their transition to mainly a terrestrial life.

Salamanders swim by, still in their eft stage; their legs already evident. Soon they will begin their next stage of land living.

I can hear the squirrels rummaging for nuts and seeds in the woods as evidenced by the rustling of leaves as they continue their ongoing search. I watch a turkey stroll by, oblivious to my presence.

The *tick . . . tick . . . tick* of falling leaves—maple, birch, and aspen—greets my ears. It is the music of the fall morning. With neither beat nor rhythm, it blends with the chirp of chickadees as they drift to the ground, unhinged from their parent tree. It's time for them to go, and their parents have released them.

I think of my parents releasing me when I was seventeen, going on eighteen. I was also set adrift with a hope and a dream. Have I achieved my dream or is it still in there, prompting me? How about you?

My first love was dance. I knew all the routines of the Mouseketeers on the Mickey Mouse Club television show and performed with them on my living room stage. In college I wanted to get my master's degree in dance, but was blocked because I lacked the required eight years of ballet training. I made a promise to myself then that wherever I went, I would offer dance classes to my students. They could find out early on if they wished to pursue a career in dance.

My second love was writing. As a child, I loved to write poems, and as an adult, I took some courses and developed some short stories worthy of publication, according to my professors. But the companies were not interested in my themes at the time, so I put them away.

Finally, after retiring from teaching and entering my later years, I became an author at age sixty-eight, the story of which is told in my first two books. Now I am publishing my third book, at age seventy, and I am still so happy writing; the words just seem to flow out of me.

The moral of the story, so to speak, is to never give up on those early dreams. They are there for a reason and could bring you great happiness. Even if life's situations prevent you from totally fulfilling them, like my dance, for example, there's a modification possible that will still bring you great satisfaction—sharing your love for it with others in some way, so they have a chance. And maybe that's what's supposed to happen, anyway, for those dreams we cannot fulfill.

~~~~~

And here I am, *writing* about it all. Experiencing a new morning in my life. Imagine that. . . .

Afternoon at My Pond

It's late afternoon at my pond; the date is October 7. A time of cold is before us, and a light but chill breeze moves through with a calming whisper.

The depth of water has fallen two and one-half feet now; scarcely two feet are left in some areas.

The surface is a mass of fallen pine needles cast off by the surrounding white pines like so much glitter, settling on the water. I look upon the display of intertwined needles; no human could have arranged such a pattern. There is a random beauty here, and I stand amazed at the sight of Nature's handiwork.

Random maple and birch leaves also dot the layer of light rust-colored pine needles like confetti, giving the sight a splash of color here and there.

The sun's rays scatter on the surface, lighting the bottom so I can see through the surface net of pine needles and leaves.

Pollywogs and efts still meander around in their diminishing home. Can they sense or even fear what's happening? *Will their legs grow out before their home dries up?* I wonder.

I look around, hearing a rustle in the woods to my left. With all the dry fallen leaves, even a scampering chipmunk can sound like a moose moving through the treescape. A snap startles me. I keep watching as a lone deer makes its way, nibbling along on its journey past the pond.

As I shift my gaze, I catch sight of a lone frog standing watch at the edge of the water. It looks like a guard, but what is it guarding? Is it the young that are swimming around encased in their tomb? Or will it be their womb from which they emerge to begin their transition to life on land?

What is Nature saying to me here, as I soak up the peace and quiet?

As I observe it all before me, I feel time slow. The message that comes is: take your time and don't rush, so you can observe the changes.

I think about the frog. It lives mainly on land but in a moist environment, chiefly water, to which it returns frequently. Yet it began its life solely in water and then grew legs and developed lungs to allow it to live on land. It is a creature that shows great adaptability.

How accepting and adaptable am I to changes that occur in *my* life? Was there ever an opportunity to go along with change that I resisted?

My thoughts go back to my brother, who was my hero, model, and true companion growing up.

When he began declining in his old age and even a little before, I didn't think he was as ill as he was. I missed my chances of spending quality time with him because I was *too busy* to notice or *didn't want* to notice how he was changing for fear of what that meant. We were in touch, but I didn't take the time to *make* time for us to be together. Before I knew it, he had passed on, and I can never get that time back.

Sometimes we don't observe changes because we're too young or too immature to notice. And then there are those of us who are quite task-oriented, also.

My brother's passing made me realize that I sometimes become so distracted by what I feel I *should* do and *need* to do that I miss seeing what's happening around me. Maybe I can begin to identify the sources of "should" in my life and eliminate some.

Why do I feel I "should" do something? Sometimes it's due to my upbringing, such as the idea that I should remember peoples' birthdays. When I forget, I may feel guilty. Now what I do is send the card when I remember or give a belated wish by phone. I take a positive action and cut off the negative feeling before it can take over.

Sometimes I "should" do something because it will bring attention to me. Maybe I want to be noticed or I'm seeking praise for a thoughtful act. I need a pat on the back; my ego needs a boost. There is a selfish undercurrent in this case.

Maybe it's my intuition prompting the act. By making someone else happy, *I* feel happy, and it takes my mind off my own troubles.

Sometimes I feel I "should" do something because I feel I have a social responsibility to do something or it will aid my physical health, mental health, or personal growth. Then there is the prospect of doing something for relaxation or enjoyment.

These are all reasons for feeling we "should" do something. Some are more acceptable than others. Some have positive results, and some have negative results. The problem comes when the "should" becomes the focus. We then can become driven to accomplish all the things we feel we ought to. Instead, we need to realize our limits and become selective in what we can accomplish, healthily.

When I overstep my limits, stress is the result; I become tired and grouchy, snapping at my loved ones. My blood pressure increases, muscles tighten, and digestive issues abound. My physical body lets me know, but sometimes my mental head-talk persists and I ignore the physical signs. I become irritable and can even become depressed if I keep up my hectic pace long enough.

Eventually, I get sick. It may be just a cold or it may be that a chronic condition develops or resurfaces. My body is in a state of dis-ease. It is crying out to be heard, and I *need* to listen.

Physically, we can get sick, but the issue of "should" can take us even further into our psychological health. Positive acts such as needing to continually give gifts to people can become addictive, as can positive behaviors such as needing to see certain people daily, outside of family members. The key here is the phrase "needing to." Needing to is a sign that there is something the person lacks. Is it attention? Or friends? Or affirmation?

The word "addiction" makes most of us think of hard drugs, cigarettes, and alcohol. But I have found myself addicted to *other* things instead. I have found addiction to be a strong habit that's tough to break. There is a tense, driven quality about it that begins to control you and can become an ingrained behavior pattern.

I was creating potpourri for a friend's pottery shop. I created blends of essential oils to use as the scents and went to the woods for the substance of my natural potpourri. It was exciting as I configured chips of white pine cones that a squirrel had piled in its dissection of them, looking for seeds to forage. I added bits and pieces of white birch bark that had been cast off. I dried wild rose petals and the shed winged seeds of maple trees. It was fun and I enjoyed the task of creating pleasing potpourri, naturally.

Then one day I realized that I couldn't enjoy a peaceful walk in the woods anymore. I was driven to collect whatever Nature had discarded in my path. Without realizing it, I had crossed over a line—a line between an enjoyable activity of collection and a *need* to collect whatever I saw. I had an intense drive; I could feel myself tighten; I was no longer calmed by my walk in Nature. I wanted to find more and more things to feel satisfied. Desire had transitioned to *need*.

I was not putting a harmful substance into my body, but I was still causing it harm. I had lost control over part of my life. Every hike had become a search. I could no longer *choose* to take a relaxed hike in Nature. My choices had become limited. And my freedom had been stolen. I was beginning to become addicted to collecting for my potpourri. As silly as it may sound, it was a big realization for me. It helped me to understand how addiction can happen.

So, what did I do? I told my friend that I would no longer be making potpourri for her shop. It took a while for me not to notice some nice things that could be collected, but gradually I returned to normal and again enjoyed a relaxed walk in the woods. And, believe me, I certainly was tempted many times to begin collecting again. I took the time to admire items but always returned them to where they had been previously lying before I picked them up.

Desire can transition to habit. Habit can transition to need. Need can transition to addiction. But we can stop the process at any time if we recognize what's happening and change it.

Another addiction I had for a while was visiting a couple who were friends. It became a routine to stop in every day for a little while after work. For me, they supplied not only friendship but acceptance, caring, support, and respect, which I didn't feel I was getting in a relationship I was having. I knew I was getting my "fix" for the day. I would leave feeling appreciated and my mood was elevated by the emotional "fix."

We know we're addicted when our enjoyable activity transforms to a *need* we don't feel we can do without. After realizing this, I knew that if I kept it up, it would eventually have a negative effect on the friendship. I began to decrease the frequency of the visits.

I think of people-pleasers. They can lose sight of who they really are or fail to discover who they really are as they seek to be what everyone else seems to think they *should* be and do what everyone else feels they *should* do.

I was that way once. And it was a frustrating, no-win situation. I kept feeling I was constantly failing, and I couldn't live up to that image of who I was supposed to be. It took years before I discovered that my failure was due to the fact that I *wasn't* that person. And that was okay. I needed to discover who I really was.

We need to be careful with the "should" in our life and honestly look at our addictions, too.

And as Nature showed me at my pond: Slow down . . . don't rush . . . observe the changes. And adapt. Take the change one step at a time.

~~~~~~~

Are you adapting to the changes that occur in your life or resisting them? Look for a positive effect of the change. Find one positive and more will follow. Is a source of "should" thinking affecting your acceptance of the change?

Is there anything you feel you *can't do without*? Remember, you can change the process of developing an addiction by first identifying it and adapting to a change. Let Nature show you how. Stay open and listen. . . .

Evening at My Pond

A week after I observed the frog "sentinel," mid-October has crept in with its changes. The light is lessening as I approach my pond. Colors dance among the clouds on the horizon, as the setting sun casts its shadow through the forest.

It is evening, and all is quiet as I move around the edges of my pond again. Not a breath of air stirs the leaves. As daytime creatures settle for the night, a quieting stillness begins to descend.

As I emerge from the evergreen forest near my home, the pond takes center stage. My first impression is of the way everything seems to be closing down for the night. The water is still and dark. I glance around for a random frog, but none appear; they are, I assume, tucked away from nighttime predators.

I lower myself to the wooden boardwalk over the far end of the pond and let my legs dangle toward the water. On occasion, when I sit here, my feet touch the cold spring water and numb almost instantly—but not today. The water level has dropped even more, a result of the long dry spell we're experiencing.

Two chickadees alight on a branch nearby. Their familiar *"chick-a-dee-dee-dee"* never ceases to warm my heart.

To my right, I watch two red squirrels scamper to the edge of the pond to get one last fill-up before night pulls down its dark shade over the great window of the sky. There, they take a side-by-side position, with tails lengthened out behind. Their cheeks quickly wobble in and out as they drink, causing me to chuckle. I don't remember ever watching a squirrel drinking so close to me before. With their thirst quenched, they scurry on their way, chasing each other up a tree trunk to their nest of sticks and leaves high in the branches above.

As the light lessens even more, the rapid twirls and chirps of crickets begins like a background symphony of consistent and constant tone.

Pollywogs, salamander efts, squirrels, chickadees, crickets, frogs—each so different, yet all here together, living their lives. So often, sunlight falling through the water has enabled me to see clear to the bottom of the pond. The pollywogs and salamander efts seem to swim at different levels from one another, and when they change levels neither collides with the other. Yet both find shelter and sustenance in the same watery world.

It's much the same with birds. Each species builds its nest at different levels, and many times in different trees or types of tree. Some build on the ground or near the water. Yet each species can survive in the same area without interference, and there is food for all. Conflict usually occurs within a species mainly during mating time as the gents compete to catch the eye of the prettiest lady. Sound familiar? And then there's the establishing of territories or home boundaries . . . again, much the same as humans do.

There are predators about but, for the most part, different species with different coloring live together in a community of life. Within the same genus, different species live together.

Then there are humans. . . . We become separated because of different skin color, different nationalities, different religions, different dialects, different beliefs, different cultures, and different politics. We seem to easily become prejudiced against someone who is different from us. *Why is that?*

First, perhaps, is the fact that when we admire someone, we may want to be just like that person. Therefore, we may take on the same prejudice they have. If we are a member of a group, we may want to feel like we *belong* and so we take on the group's prejudice.

Children usually take on the same prejudice as their parents even though they may have had no personal experience to cause that. Parents are models to their children, and so if the parent feels that way, it must be right, even if it gives the child a "not so good" feeling inside. This will continue until some*one* or some*thing* along the way shows them a different perspective, and it releases them from the chains that have been holding them back.

In my case, it was a family member I admired who was prejudiced against a certain race of people, and so I adopted that attitude also. During my freshman year of college, there was a girl of that particular race on my wing in the dorm. I avoided her totally. But as I watched her, I came to realize that she was a pleasant person, a nice person, a giving person, and I gradually began to change my dislike of her. I could feel my prejudice lessening. And we became friends. There wasn't anything I *couldn't* like about her. I never told my family about her, though. I hadn't become strong enough yet to do so and face their disapproval.

When one person hurts another, we can understand how a dislike or disrespect can develop, but when we categorize *all* people of that specific religion, race, behavior, or belief—that's prejudice. Prejudice is a darkness that descends and colors everything in our life. Negative begets more negative; prejudice begets more prejudice. We become quite a negative and prejudiced person in more and more avenues of our life.

We can become prejudiced against certain professions. Do we feel superior to them? Why? Do we *need* to feel that way? *What* is that need? *Where* does it come from? Is it caused by a lack in us that we don't want to acknowledge? If we think of them as *below* us, does it help us feel better about ourselves? But do we really feel better—deep down . . . soul deep?

Are we prejudiced against people who are overweight or those who seem to eat everything and never gain an ounce? What about smokers or those who can't control their alcohol intake? Where do these prejudices come from?

I've spent some time at my pond thinking about my own prejudices; Nature has helped me to identify some of them without judgment and helped me to see how and why I've developed them. As an adult, I know I can now rid myself of any of them if I wish.

I ask myself, do I have a *right* to feel that prejudice? Am I *entitled* to that prejudice because of some past event? Does having that prejudice give me a happy feeling or is it a feeling of not wanting to be around them, not wanting to look at them, not wanting to acknowledge them? Is that a positive feeling? Or are my muscles tightening and my blood pressure climbing? Do I withdraw when I'm faced with my prejudice, or am I angry and unreasonable? Neither feels good.

Watching the birds at my pond and all the other creatures living peacefully in community reinforced the idea I had used with the girl on my wing in the college dormitory. I needed to get to know someone of that religion, race, belief, profession, economic class, or whatever it is that I've identified as a personal prejudice and focus on one positive thing about the person—physical characteristic, talent, skill, personality characteristic. And gradually, I would see more positives about them. Eventually, their one act or quality or characteristic that initially caused the prejudice to develop within me would take on a more minor role—if that was my desire.

> I'm at my pond, it's quiet here,
> In solitude am I,
> To be in Nature is my call,
> I seat myself and sigh.
>
> Falling leaves so lightly sit,
> Pine needles float along,
> Tree crickets have their constant chirp,
> While chickadees sing their song.
>
> For it is here that I find peace
> From worries that crowd my heart,
> Anger, loss, or grief I'm feeling—
> Here it seems to depart.
>
> For Nature is my guide, you see,
> My companion through it all,
> She's always there—my constant pal,
> Her wisdom is my draw.

Intention is the foundation of any healing. Take your intention to Nature. Let her settle you and surround you in her beauty, solitude, and peace. Listen to her wherever you are and she will guide you with her wisdom. Nature has no prejudices; she is our teacher.

Let her wisdom bring changes within you wherever they are needed.

Budding Lilac

opened my wooden entry door and stepped outside, responding to a sense of urgency. What did the Natural World have to tell me today?

Around me the maples and birches, which had long before dropped their colorful leaves, were standing naked before me. Even the golden yellow needles of the tamarack tree, more commonly known as larch, had been released and now rested on the ground. The dingy gray of the skies heralded the dark and dismal part of fall right before winter sets in. But that was quickly coming to an end. The air was still—not a whisper of wind.

The first snow had fallen last night like a light blanket of white being pulled over a sleeping babe. The dusting of flakes alighted on every blade of dying grass and every leafless twig upon the trees surrounding me.

I began my trek toward the workshop, angling past my garden. As I approached my lilac bush, I recalled its sweet-smelling lavender blossoms of last spring. And then the brown seed clusters that formed later, huddled together on the tiniest of twigs. Now it looked barren of everything except a tiny point at the end of one of the branches. *What is that?* I wondered. *It can't be a bud. Or can it?*

My attention was drawn to a light, fluffy snowflake resting on the pointed tip. Suddenly, the sun burst from behind its covering cloud, reflecting its beam on the snowflake, causing it to sparkle like a many-faceted diamond.

I drew closer and blew at it lightly. The snowflake lifted and began floating up for just a second before cascading down and coming to rest on a nearby shaft of spiraea that had made its home in the shadow of the lilac. Looking closer at the entire bush, I realized that *all* the branches had tiny points at their tips.

I began looking around and noticed for the first time, as I peered closely at the branches and twigs, that all the bushes and trees had formed their buds—the very buds that would become more colorful in the spring with the new warmth of the sun's rays.

I had always just assumed that bushes and trees budded in the spring, probably because that's when I *noticed* them. Now I knew that wasn't true. Each of these plants formed its buds by the end of fall while it was still making its own food and before its juices descended to the roots for winter. These buds were waiting for the proper moment and best conditions to do what Nature had planned for them to do—swell and burst open, yielding new stems, leaves, and flowers. And how we welcome that celebration of spring and new life.

Many of the buds on the lilac bush before me had collected numerous flakes, attached and shifting with the now stirring breeze. It made it hard to see the buds themselves. And I began to ponder the scene before me, my thoughts taking me to my own personal journey.

Sometimes I feel like the snow-covered buds. *How can that be? What am I feeling? What's the connection?* Then I begin to realize that at times I've felt that I'm muddling through life with no sense of direction; I can't see where I'm going. I feel blinded as to what to do next, just as the snow cover has blinded the bud from the sun. Then I think maybe that's the way it's supposed to be—live each day with all the surprises and challenges life has to offer, and try to live it with a smile. Greet people; be happy and joyful. But is that enough?

It made me remember a workshop I once attended. A number of people there were from my town, and then there were others I had never met. We were divided into small groups of seven or eight and directed to introduce ourselves to the group, sharing names and where we lived. Then the task was laid before us: Even if we were strangers, we were to identify one characteristic or quality we admired in each person in our group and speak it aloud.

There was one person in my group with whom I had contact many times each week. We worked in the same school and would pass each other in the hall. Whenever I saw her, I would smile a friendly greeting. She would reply, but never smile or look at me. I never heard her laugh when we were in a group. She was always quiet, controlled, and firm. That was my impression of her still after three years of working in the same school.

She was commenting now on different people in our group, and when she got to me, her words shot through me like a lightning bolt.

"Debby, your smile is like a light in the darkness."

Oh . . . my. . . .

The tears began to swell in my eyes, threatening to tumble out and splash in my lap. What was I feeling? Embarrassment? Overwhelmed? I was shocked, truly moved by the compliment she had just given me so honestly and sincerely. Then she moved on to the person beside me.

I reveled in the moment—truly a "wow."

It made me realize that we don't always know how we affect others just by being the people we are and sharing our gifts. It just happens with no pretense or intention on our parts. It's a natural, unconscious occurrence, and people are "touched." It made me aware that my smile gives people a lift. It's a positive thing.

We hold many gifts within us just waiting to burst forth like the bud on my lilac, but the greatest gift of all is what we do *naturally*. If we like to sing, sing to a child and watch how she's lulled to sleep. A babe finds peace and comfort in her Mother's voice. We don't have to be trained singers. We have only to *like* to do it. The singing brings peace to the child and brings joy to us. How many people sing in the shower or hum as they work?

The promise held within the bud for the entire winter is for the stem, leaves, and flowers that appear in the spring and the eventual seeds that the bud produces for new life to begin.

Fall is past; spring is future. Nature's cycle of the seasons is there to teach us. For every ending, there is a new beginning. Each year we let the fall go and welcome the hope of spring.

Are there things in your life that have ended, that you've had to let go of? Remember, in between fall and spring, there is always winter—sometimes long, seemingly without end, and cold; sometimes shorter and easier—but always part of the cycle of life. Our new beginning does not come immediately after an ending. It takes time and patience. A new beginning takes feeding and watering to sprout, and then it needs cultivation to grow and blossom.

~~~~~~

Do you focus on what's falling and left behind like the colorful autumn leaves now fading on the ground? Or do you look ahead with hope to a new spring, filled again with the buds of new birth? It's a choice only you can make.

Have you found a new beginning?

winter

The allure of winter—
  . . .crispness
    . . .clarity
Let us go deeper into winter:

The sharpness of the diamonds,
  sparkling in the snow,
Reflections of moon glow
  on the ice-covered fields,
Pointing us in new directions
  from which to grow,
Holding the beauty within—
  . . .reds,
    . . .blues,
      . . .yellows,

Heralding the spring to come
  after the rest, the calm,
Bursting forth with newness—
  rejuvenation.

Storm

took another step into the stinging sleet that pelted my face and body. Leaning into the wind, step by step, I forged my way down the woodland path.

My muscles felt tightened and constricted. With my head bent well into my puffy goose down jacket, I lowered my entire body, pushing with my boots against the accumulated snow adrift on the trail.

Why am I even out here? What am I trying to prove? I had wanted to experience the tougher side of Nature and read the message there. Well, here I was.

The winds seemed to grab at me, pushing me backwards, yet I journeyed on, albeit at a much slower pace than before.

It was winter in the Adirondack Mountains, and I was caught hiking in the midst of a raging snowstorm about a half-mile from home. The wind chill was forcing the temperatures well below zero.

I had yearned to experience the biting sensation of ice bits stinging my face, taking my breath away. Well, that's exactly what was happening now. My breath began coming in shortened gasps.

This was another side of Nature's energies—not that of beauty or color, but a somewhat scary side. What was it telling me?

I felt stressed as I plowed forward, and fear began to creep in.

It was a challenge to look at this experience as gift. And yet Nature had always been about gift to me, about gifting me freely with its wonderful qualities and wisdom. *Can I still see the gift even in this experience?*

I felt cold and wet and scared at the turbulence. The wind had begun to howl as it increased in velocity. Sleet and snow were pelting the tree branches, forcing them to bend and sway and tossing them about. Creaking and cracking sounds broke through the howl as trees lost their limbs and frozen branches were forced to tremble.

I continued to push forward, placing one foot in front of the other, as I made my way toward home. *Another half mile to go. I can do this. I can make it.*

Then an intensely powerful gust of wind stopped me in my tracks, making it impossible for me to move forward another step. It was as if Nature were saying—stop! That's far enough. Listen to me.

I was taking a big risk being out in such a violent storm. *What if a limb broke off and knocked me over? What if I slipped and fell, striking my head on a boulder hidden beneath the snow? When would anyone find me? Risk . . . risk . . . was that the message?*

As the gust of wind lessened, I noticed an uprooted spruce tree beside the trail. Hunkering down beneath the root mass to rest, my mind jumped into gear. I asked myself, *Do I enjoy taking risks or do I shy away and succumb to the status quo? I did choose to come out here today instead of staying protected in my warm house away from the battering winds and ice. But usually?*

Life is full of risks, some of which are life-threatening. I never thought of myself as a big risk-taker. I enjoy having a plan and a supposed outcome to begin with. Obviously, changes may occur along the way, but usually I've done my research, considered my options, and made some decisions. All of this had minimized the risk I was about to take.

There are degrees of risk-taking. I have found that when I wish to invest money, I steer away from the stock market where there are high stakes. I am more comfortable earning a lower return that's more consistent and a bit more secure. I prefer to "play it safe" *versus* "take the chance." That probably goes back to some childhood experiences.

I took a risk when I was diagnosed with Multiple Sclerosis. I could have rallied, as some did, to adopting the "attack the invader" mode. Instead, I chose a quieter mode of accepting the diagnosis, grieving the news, and giving my body the support it needed to begin healing.

I began to analyze my negative stresses and increase my knowledge and understanding of the disease. I adapted my lifestyle to read my body before my exercise regimen, incorporating yoga at the very least and always a walk in Nature. It was a more calming and quiet approach rather than being driven to attack the culprit.

Give me the strength to endure became my mantra. I applied my energies in a more positive way, and I feel it increased the probability of a positive outcome.

When we are on the attack, our "fight or flight" response kicks in, whether it's our own self-expectations driving us or a major crisis. Our adrenalin production increases and our muscles tense in preparation, driving blood inward to protect our vital organs. Over a prolonged period of time, this level of anxiety can work against us. We've constructed one of our own barriers or "life bars" to living healthily and being able to share our gifts. The stress we've taken on accumulates to a point where we are overwhelmed. We want to quit. We can't take it anymore. We are driving ourselves, and our body responds accordingly. With me, it was an exacerbation of Multiple Sclerosis. Someone else might develop high blood pressure or arteriosclerosis. Whatever it is, our body will react. Then it's time for us to sit up and take notice of what we're doing to ourselves.

So, what was Nature's message to me through this snowstorm?

It was to recognize and begin to dismantle my own barriers to living healthily. There is risk involved in doing so. Take the risk and walk through the storms in life and look for the sun to break through. Even in negative times, when the ice is pelting me and the wind chills me to the bone, Nature is there to support and guide me through it all.

The winds had died down and the snowfall was letting up as I emerged from my hideaway. It would be a much easier hike back to my house now. The sun caught my eye, having popped out as the clouds performed a mass exit. The risk had been worth it. I had heard Nature's whispered message, even in a snowstorm.

~~~~~

What kind of a risk-taker are you?

It's to our benefit to take the risk of recognizing and dismantling our own life barriers.

What holds *you* back?

A Moment in Time

opened my eyes to the sunlight streaming in through the window. As I lifted my sleep-ridden body from the bed, I became aware of a glistening effect outside the window. What was it? The brightness of it was drawing me closer. I felt as if I was being pulled like the tide coming into shore. But by what?

When I got to the window, my eyes searched the landscape. And then I saw it. It had been raining when I went to bed, even though it was January in the Adirondacks. The rain had stopped during the night and the temperatures dropped.

My gaze lighted on a single, ice-covered cherry tree, now barren of leaves. It was radiating a glistening aura as the angled rays of the rising sun shone through the ice, which was coating the entire tree. Grabbing the binoculars from the stand near the window, I focused on the air surrounding the tree. I could actually see colorful droplets of frozen water vapor circling in the air. Yellow, blue, green, red—everywhere I saw the rainbow colors in the air, though with the naked eye, I would have missed that.

I stood in awe at Nature's gift to me at that moment, embracing it in totality.

As I watched, the wind gently nudged a light covering of nearby clouds. Flowing over the sun, haziness replaced the brilliant direct rays of earlier. The sight began to dull.

And then it was gone.

I had seen the snow sparkling like a field of diamonds many times and reflecting off tree branches. But this was like the light was coming from *within* the tree itself and was shining outward. It was glistening with an inner glow for all to see . . . or for *me* to see—a moment in time I could have easily missed.

I'll never forget the glow of that tree—so different from anything I have ever witnessed before or since. I stood there thinking, *Life is made up of moments like these. And they're so quickly gone.* I had been reminded to take the time to notice, to see, to grab the moment. Then—to recognize the gift and let it rest in my heart, enriching my soul.

I began to think about how busy we can get. We miss these moments, and yet they're everywhere. But where is our focus?

My soulmate, Gary, latches on to Nature's gifts, showing me his finds most every day, where many times I still miss the opportunities to see and touch what Nature offers. I realize that with my tendency toward busyness indoors and a life involving a focus on tasks, I also need to take the opportunity to view the marvels before me—the gifts all around. They are always there for me to see and touch and hold.

It only takes a moment for the butterfly to totally exit its chrysalis and experience a new life. Finally free from the encapsulation in which it has existed for two or three weeks, it is now ready for its first flight to a tree branch to await the drying of its wings.

It only takes a moment for the blossom of the Apostle plant to fully open before it begins the slow transition of curling and drying.

And it only takes a moment for a child to take her first step. There's only one first. We can't repeat it. We're either there when it happens or we're not. And we can't get it back.

Many a parent has longed to catch the excitement that fills the air when a child discovers moving upright. And it only happens once—in a moment.

~~~~~~

Look around and capture the moments—each moment—Nature's gift to you.

Take some time and remember *your* special moments in life.

View the setting. See the colors. Listen to the sounds. Inhale the fragrances. Experience the feelings. Take a deep breath.

And let your heart and soul breathe, too.

Fog

~~~~

It had rained most of the night even though it was the middle of winter in the Adirondack Mountains of New York State and the precipitation is usually snow. Lots of snow. The below-zero temperatures we had been having had spiked to forty degrees *above* zero during the nighttime hours.

Now it was seven a.m. Looking out the window in my living room, I could see a blanket of dense fog covering the valley before me. The east branch of the Au Sable River wove its way, meandering through the valley banked by the Jay Range of mountains that stood rising in the distance—staunch and stately.

I love this view. I give thanks for the blessing it has provided me every day since I purchased this land more than fifteen years ago. My little house is nestled on the side of a small mountain directly opposite the Jay Range.

Now as I stood here looking out yet again, I marveled at the sight. Down below me was a hay field that was periodically cut and baled for the neighboring farms. Today, however, it was covered with snow—a *total* blanket of white.

Usually, the fog appeared light and wispy—quite transparent. Not today. I couldn't remember ever seeing the fog this dense across the field. If I had been standing in it, I'm not sure I could even have seen my hand in front of my face. Only once before had I been in fog this thick, this dense.

Years back, I was bent on becoming a "46er," meaning someone who has climbed all forty-six of the High Peaks in the Adirondack Mountains. Although I was now in my little house looking out as an observer, I well remember the sensations and emotions I experienced on my climb up one of those peaks, Nippletop Mountain.

I hiked alone in those days, not knowing anyone at the time who enjoyed the same kind of activity. I had started out with my backpack, which contained water, a guide book, and lunch. Also tucked inside a pouch were first-aid supplies and my whistle in case I had to send out an S-O-S.

The day was cloudy and warm, and the hiking was going well at first. I fell into my pace, loving what I was doing.

The trail became more challenging; my breathing quickened. I passed through mistiness as I made my way to the top of the mountain; it was as if a very thin cloud had settled there. I'd often seen clouds shrouding the peaks from down below, but I'd never been within a cloud before. It was kind of eerie, but I grew accustomed to it as I continued on, and had no trouble seeing where I was going.

As I began the final ascent, I became aware that the fog had gotten thicker—more dense, more solid. I began to feel isolated but not scared. *Just a new experience for me,* was my thought. I slowed my pace and found myself looking down a lot more as I moved along the trail. I had to remind myself to periodically look up to keep sight of the circular trail markers that identified the way to the top.

Caution . . . caution . . . *Do I turn back? I have to be almost there.*

I was alone in the fog, yet I felt safe. A comforting sense enveloped me—*I'm all wrapped up in a cozy blanket, a blanket of fog.* I could see the droplets in the air around me enveloping me, caressing me, encasing me in their beauty—exquisite.

I slowed my pace even more. My senses became increasingly acute as my field of sight lessened. The air was still; all the usual birdsongs were silent. I could feel the delicate droplets of moisture landing on my skin—my face, my arms, my legs. It was refreshing. I could smell the dampness of the vegetation around me. The trees gave off the mixed scents of pine and balsam while the dampened earth exuded a fragrance all its own.

I crossed a lower area where moisture had collected over time. Stepping carefully lest my hiking boots become saturated, I must have brushed against a tree's lower limb that lay hidden by the fog. It surprised me, my sense of touch alerted once again.

I stopped and closed my eyes, wanting to immerse myself in the moment. I was floating in the quiet atmosphere of being held and supported. I was suspended above the earth, becoming one with the fog.

I can't describe the view from the peak of Nippletop Mountain, for I never saw one. Yet I remember my experience to this day. Forever, it is implanted in my mind and lives on in my cells. My experience was unique and memorable—*love that fog!*

Now, as I stood in my living room, gazing out at the blanket of fog before me and remembering my climb, my thoughts focused on how dense the layer of fog can become. Today both the field and the river were totally shielded from my view, the fog shrouding them like a veil. I could no longer see the exposed boulders that protruded midstream in the river or the eroded banks here and there. The willows that usually leaned outward over the water were obliterated. Even the holes in the river bank were filled in by the lacy, floating, settling fog.

It was as if I could draw a line between where the upper border of white ended and the wooded mountains began. As clear as ever, they were illuminated by the now brilliant sun, rising above the distant horizon. I was struck by the contrast and the beauty of it all. I felt settled. I felt calmed. *Have there been other times in my life when I've felt this calm?*

Time passed as I searched through my bank of memories. I felt mesmerized, as if I were in a trance.

As I came out of my reverie, I focused again on the fog before me. As I did so, it began creeping to the left, reacting to the changes in air temperatures. With the water holding its cold temperatures, the air was warming and beginning to move. Eventually it would dissipate, but the potential for it to occur again, *under the right conditions*, would remain.

There was another message for me here, besides the sense of calm the fog had provided me. But what was it?

I had observed the fog, likening it to a veil, covering everything physically visible. But what about a mind-veil? Isn't the world we see affected by our past experiences, joys, failures, disappointments, judgements, attitudes? Don't we see our world through the veil before our mind? So we're not really present to what's there; we're seeing it through our past experiences.

It is one of the great works of emotional/spiritual adulthood to recognize the fog through which we see the world and to clear it.

~~~~~

How has your mind-veil affected your actions, reactions, or attitudes about someone or something?

As the fog is cleared by the warmth of the sun shining through, so you can lift *your* veil and allow the warmth of a new understanding and perspective to glow within you.

13

My World at
Twenty Degrees Below Zero

~~~~

piled on my clothes, layer upon layer, in preparation for the cold temperatures outside. I donned my blue down coat over snow pants, grabbed my heavy insulated gloves, and wrapped my woolen scarf around my neck to keep out the cold. *There. Guess I'm all set.*

Glancing at the thermometer, I gasped. "Twenty degrees below zero. You've got to be kidding!" I hadn't seen temperatures like that in many years.

As I approached the door, I noticed the metal knob was covered in frost. Grabbing it with a gloved hand, I began to turn it, feeling the resistance. Then, with more effort, I yanked the door, and it creaked open on complaining hinges.

The frigid air struck my face with a cutting bitterness. I stood there in the quiet . . . in the stillness . . . in the silence. All of Nature seemed to be shrouded in ice and snow. *This is my home. This is my world,* I thought.

I took my first step, hearing a loud crunch as the accumulated snow gave way beneath my weight. I took a few more steps, noticing the sharpness of the sound as my steps broke up the crystalline structure of the snow. It was different—hard to describe.

When the snow is wet, it can be more of a dull, sloshing sound as the crystals begin their melt down. When it's dry, there's more of a light, fluffy sound, hardly noticeable at all. When it's this cold, I can only describe it as a squeaky, squealing sound as the frozen crystals resist the movement, as if they're competing with one another to hold their stance.

Not a needle was stirring on the pines outside my door, projecting an eerie stillness to the scene. The only air movement was my breath. As I exhaled, I watched my breath become crystalline before my face and vividly hang as if suspended in thin air. I felt my nostrils sticking together, resisting another intake of frigid air. I quickly tried to raise my scarf to cover my nose, struggling to grasp it with my gloved hand. With that accomplished, I took another step.

My eyes were beginning to tear and cloud my view, though I could still see enough to walk. As the tears released, they froze on my skin. I raised my scarf even higher on my face and eventually felt the tears thaw and soak into my scarf.

Looking around, I saw the trees standing as if locked in a stiffened stance. It was as if all time had stopped. I found the stillness disquieting. This world—*my* world—was speaking loudly to me of contraction and withdrawal.

I heard a loud *crack*. Then—*snap*. I stopped abruptly, my whole body on alert. I braced for another sudden sharp sound, but it didn't come—at least not now. I'd been moving along slowly—chopping along—feeling stiff out here. The cracking, snapping sounds had been caused by the liquid in the trees expanding as it froze in these extreme temperatures. It made me think about how fragile the world *feels*; how fragile the world *is*; how easily it could *shatter*.

My thoughts were jarred to times I had been cold to others—when I had shut them out, withdrawing into myself. But why? Was I feeling their invasion of my privacy—getting too close to me? Was I in need of *preserving* my core—my *self*? Did I need to *protect* something within myself? Was I fearful of something?

I stood there realizing that I have been cold to others out of a need to protect my *self*. And, contrarily, I have had others project coldness toward me. In those instances, I had felt ignored, unimportant, insignificant, not valued.

It was as if they said, without speaking a word, "You are not worthy of my time or notice. You are nothing in my eyes."

Is that the message I want to convey to others?

Nature had given me yet another insight into my behaviors—another behavior I wanted to modify. I might be cool towards someone who has earned my distrust or who was argumentative; that reaction goes back to my childhood experiences. But I needed to be honest about what message I *wanted* to communicate and *why* I had that reaction at all. That would take some thought and quiet time.

I decided I did not want to project the coldness of twenty degrees below zero. The underlying cause of the reaction itself needed to be identified and understood. Once

I understood, I was free to change my reaction. Since change is synonymous with life, I'd consequently feel a little more alive! Another memory comes into focus. . . .

There was a woman who I felt uncomfortable being around. The reason was she used profanity in just about every sentence she spoke. It reminded me of my dad cursing and swearing at my mom when I was growing up. The yelling had always scared me. Still, this woman's swearing bothered me, and I began to distance myself from her. Then I started to notice that she had some positive qualities, too, so I decided to focus on those.

One day when I was ill, she came to my aid. We began meeting and talking, and over time became quite good friends. It was then that I realized her swearing no longer bothered me. My father's swearing was always done in anger. With my friend, it was part of her everyday vocabulary. That was different. Yet my previous experience had caused me to have a negative reaction to her initially.

In my opinion, it takes a lifetime for us to grow up—a lifetime to grow beyond greed, belittling of others in thought or action, the selfish acts we at times delve into. A lifetime to grow closer to the unselfish, caring, generous, and loving people we were meant to be.

~~~~~~~

Are there people you have been cold to in your life—those who are getting the "twenty below treatment" from you? What was it about them that triggered your reaction? Was it *them* or something in *you*?

Remember that cold temperatures rise; everything warms; spring comes again. Look to Nature and focus on her beauty. Feel her support of your dilemma. Let her insights awaken within you.

And listen. . . .

Allow her peace to enter in.

Winter Walk in the Forest

love to walk in the snow in the wintertime. The soft fluff of snow flies off my boots with each step I take. The path before me is a cloak of white, meandering through the woods. I am an explorer into untrodden territory.

Discovery is at my door.

After a few minutes of forging my way through the snow, I arrive at one of my favorite places—my seat. It's an old, brown vinyl bus seat that we placed here years ago, providing a comfortable resting spot for our aging bones. I seat myself, resting my walking poles against the trunk of a nearby pine tree. This seat is on the side of a hill with a clear view of the tree-covered hills ahead, blending into the steeper mountains in the distance. They look like rounded steps to a monument in the clouds. White mist hides the apex of the view, covering it like a shroud.

The day is warm for winter, around thirty degrees Fahrenheit. The sky above me is a bright blue, with the sun shining boldly. Only the distant white shroud holds the promise of precipitation. There's little air movement as I sit . . . as I wait. . . .

After quite a while, something moves, and I see them. Two deer begin their approach down below me, quietly making their way up the small hill where I sit. They stay in the pine forest where there isn't much snow cover. Moving slowly, they pause here and there to nibble a tasty treat from the forest floor.

I can see their coats—chocolate brown—thickly hugging their bodies to protect against winter's sometimes frigid temps. Their tails are solid black trimmed with bright white on top. When startled, these deer flip up their tails, showing the bright white coloring underneath from whence they get their name—Whitetail Deer. One of the deer has a deep brown streak extending from its eyes all the way down to the tip of its nose. It's so dark it's almost black and quite distinctive. This is the one most familiar to me.

When deer visit me often, I am reminded of my creative adventures. It's as if they come to give me support and encouragement. I feel a surge of confidence as I think of my writing endeavors.

Okay, you're telling me I'm supposed to continue writing, even though I sometimes want to quit. I get it. Thank you. I'll persist.

They stop in their wanderings and look up at me. Our eyes connect and we gaze at one another. The solid black pupils of their eyes seem to completely fill their eye sockets.

"You're beautiful," I say to them. They seem to understand my words as they nod their heads and continue on.

When the deer have gone, I get up from my seat and continue my walk. In no time at all, I see a paw print in the snow. I squat down to take a closer look.

I see evidence of five toes on each of four prints, with two of the prints overlapping each other; the pattern continues in a line. Some prints are larger, especially where the sun peeks in among the tree branches to cause a melt.

I got it—fox, I think.

Sunlight is wonderful on this winter's day. It brightens me; it cheers me; and certainly lifts my spirits. The effect is indeed positive.

My walk continues to a marshy area where the waters pool into a tiny makeshift pond whose only inhabitants are a couple of frogs in the summer. A tiny spring feeds the marshy area that recedes each fall to a puddle, sometimes drying up completely.

Some water has collected from our thaws and drained to this low area. Now the pooled water is frozen solid.

Since we've had a number of thaws this winter, I can see leaves and pine needles encased in the ice at various levels. Some are at the top, others a ways down, still others barely visible at all. Each layer speaks loudly of catching the errant leaf, cast off and blown by the wind to rest here, unsuspecting of its future entrapment.

I'm struck by the coloring of the frozen water, attributing some of the cause to the hovering pines surrounding the area. The outer ring of ice is clear in color to the bank where it adheres, totally transparent. Within that ring lies another smaller ring of solid white outlined by a yellowish line that borders another even smaller ring of a duller white, again outlined by a yellowish line. And so it goes—I count five rings finally ending in the center with a larger frozen pool of pale yellow.

I suspect the pine needles are responsible for the

yellowish hue. When the old dry needles turn a rust color, they are shed throughout fall and winter. They drop into the tiny pond and begin to decay, eliciting the yellowish tinge I see. The water then freezes. Time passes and the next thaw arrives, accompanied by a little rain. Temperatures drop and the water freezes again. But each thaw is here depicted—the cycle of thawing and freezing shown explicitly before me, allowing me to see deeply into the pond's shallows.

As I gaze at the oval before me, I think of the life lines of love. Each line is continual yet appears wavy at times, like relationships. All relationships have their ups and downs, ins and outs.

Love can heal us; the lack of love can destroy our spirit.

Holding that thought, I turn from the tiny pond and begin to make my way home.

Love . . . love . . . love . . . .

~~~~~~

Have you ever felt trapped like the leaves in a frozen pond, unable to move, unable to grow, unable to be heard?

And did you finally experience the melt of spring and find yourself floating to a new life?

Woodpecker Holes in Winter

The day was overcast with a snowfall prediction of six inches. Now there was a slight dusting of white covering our dirt driveway. As I made the first tracks in the snow on my trek, I began to wonder what surprises I might encounter today. Nature always had something in store.

As I turned the corner, I became aware of a hammering sound not far away. It was quite repetitive, which made me realize it must be a woodpecker. It was loud enough to be a Pileated Woodpecker.

These are the largest of the woodpecker species, being about the size of a crow with a black back and a bright red crest on the head. Their gray bill can excavate long, oval holes in a tree up to several feet in length. I had seen a pair of them flitting from dead tree to dead tree at the edge of the driveway not long ago.

As I stopped to listen more closely, the sound continued without a pause. *You must have found a really good tree there— lots of insects for you,* I thought. Standing there, I focused on where the sound was coming from. *Maybe I'll try to find the tree on my way back.*

The steady, quick rhythm of the hammering I was hearing indicated that the bird was on a quest for food. If the strikes were slow and intermittent, the bird would be declaring territorial boundaries. At times, I had heard that also.

It's amazing to me how quickly woodpeckers can hammer, their necks strong yet flexible. There was a hollowness to the sound I was hearing, implying the dead or dying tree was probably missing its core altogether.

I walked on, leaving the drilling behind.

I often walk to the end of our dirt and gravel road as a regular hike each day. Today, I turned around at the end and began my way back, wondering if I'd still hear the now familiar hammering. When I approached the area where I first encountered the hammering, all was now quiet.

I decided to take one of the side paths we had made on the property in the direction of the hammering I'd heard. Through the brush and berry bushes, past a few small birches and struggling pines, the snow-covered path guided me farther up the hill. My eyes continually searched for a ravaged tree trunk with freshly drilled holes.

Then I saw it.

The dry, gray trunk stood about twenty feet tall. The rest of the tree had long ago lost its branches and leaves to time. Even the top had been toppled by rot years ago. Worm trails adorned the trunk, now devoid of all its bark.

The remaining trunk in front of me stood as the main character in Nature's four-act play. It had once been a seedling, developing into a young tree followed by adulthood, and finally old age had claimed it until the end of its life. I closed my eyes, imagining the beauty of the tree in its vibrant years—lofty branches of green leaves, swaying in the gentle breeze.

After a few moments, I opened my eyes, coming out of my reverie. Staring at the tree, I realized there were holes drilled everywhere. *You must be housing an abundance of insects and worms,* I thought. *Lucky, the woodpeckers that find you.*

I was witness to Nature's cycle of growth and death. Before me, it all became clear, *very* clear. And how even in *our* dying, the potential is there to provide a life for others through the wisdom that is shared and a realization of the finality of life as we know it. But the person who we were goes on within the hearts and memories of others. Think of how being present to another in their elder years allows us a new perspective on our life or end of life. A dying tree provides a home for the insects that are food for the birds that go forth and feed their young. Do we not feed our young through *our* dying—through wisdom—through memories? I never thought of death in that way before.

As I examined the tree, I noticed that some of the drilled holes were gray and dry, obviously older ones. But then there were the fresh ones—large ones—eight or nine inches long and drilled to the very core of the tree. The drilled wood was colored shades of gold and peach and orange. I never knew old decayed wood could be so colorful . . . so pretty.

An abundance of sawdust and wood chips cascaded down the trunk to where a pile had collected at the base on top of the snow. I removed my gloves. The dust was soft and surprisingly damp as I ran my hand across it. Picking some up, I held it in my open hand and smelled it. The mild scent was of freshly cut wood. Again, I was surprised; I never knew dead wood could retain a lingering scent. It wasn't as strong as fresh-cut red cedar or balsam might be, but it was still faintly there. Most trees are cut when they are alive for lumber and such, but this trunk was dead—quite dead, yet retaining some of its once-dominant scent.

Any bugs that had been there were gone; I could not find a single one. *A very thorough feeder,* I thought. I began to think of the benefit dead trees provide for woodpeckers and sapsuckers by housing the insects they need to survive. Also, they give larger birds a place to roost, unencumbered by leaves and branches of needles to block their view of additional food.

Nature takes care of her own and the cycle goes on and on. A tree dies, providing a home for insects that attract birds to feed on them and at the same time speed the disintegration of the core. The sawdust and wood chips will become fertilizer for new trees and plants to grow. And the forest goes on. . . .

From death does new life spring up.

What is the message here? That all is of a purpose in Nature. No one part is more important than another. And Nature shows no favoritism.

Why, then, do some people strive to feel they're more important than others—*better* than others?

We are all important in the scheme of things, yet we have different roles, different jobs so to speak. As Nature shows, we are each as important as another.

Remembering how *we* were made to feel is the motivation for *not* treating others in a demeaning way. We don't have to *like* everyone, but finding it in our hearts to *respect* others is the key to peace.

~~~~~~~~

Did someone in your past try to make you feel of less importance than them?

Remembering your feelings at the time, did you allow them to succeed?

Let a quiet walk in Nature remind you of your place in the family of all things.

16

Winter Feast

I sit down at my kitchen table each morning for breakfast and stare out the window that I'm facing as I eat. Today, I'm watching the darkened clouds floating across the sky—*not in any rush this morning,* I think. Some days they scurry as if they're racing toward a finish line somewhere. At other times, I see the snowflakes drifting by the window, depending on the season. In summer, I listen to the rain pelting down as it strikes and runs down the pane of glass before me.

Springtime heralds a great deal of activity in the bird world with mating rituals, the search for nesting sites, and the feeding of hatchlings. I can watch the entire performance with the actors and actresses right outside my window.

But now it's pretty quiet. It's winter, and most of the birds hunker down except on bright, sunny days when they ravage for food.

So I pull out my chair and seat myself, not expecting to see much besides the clouds and maybe some snowflakes drifting by. I find myself carefully lowering my body to this seat on wheels—my grandson's delight. I notice the branches on the trees outside are moving slightly, stirred by a somewhat gentle breeze.

Before me is a steaming bowl of cooked millet. I've seen little balls of grain like these in bags of bird food in the store, but I never thought of ingesting any myself until some years ago. I found a recipe and tried it out—delicious!

I came to find out that these little balls of grain are quite nutritious, providing niacin, thiamin, and zinc, besides being high in antioxidants. That cinched it for me as another breakfast option.

When I cook millet in a combination of milk and water, I add a little flax meal, some sunflower seeds, and raisins, and serve it with warmed milk and honey. Not bad at all for a healthy breakfast.

As I pick up my spoon, movement outside the window catches my eye. I can't believe it! There are three ruffed grouse sitting on the thin branches of the staghorn sumac out front. The birds are quite large and look somewhat overbearing as they rest on the skinny, erratically branching twigs with their feathers fluffed out against the harsh winter temperatures. *What in the world?*

Then I realize what they're doing. They're eating the seeds that are clustered in the wine-colored clumps at the tips of each tiny branch—the hairy covered extension of last year's new growth. The shrub is well named, for the branches do look like the antlers of a deer in velvet, especially now, when they are barren of leaves.

Those leaves are a gorgeous array of color in the fall—a mass of green to yellow to orange to red to purple and all shades in between. I've taken many a picture of them.

I've observed the male staghorn sumac producing greenish-yellow lacy flowers in the spring. The female of the species produces the wine-red clusters of berries after pollination. The male and the female are different plants, unlike some trees that house both male and female on the same one, such as the white pine.

The normally green leaves of the sumac are covered with tiny hairs and are very soft to the touch. Deer enjoy them, too. I've seen deer standing on their hind legs for up to ten seconds to nibble the tender tips right on top, over and over again. I've watched them feast right outside my window.

More movement catches my eye as the grouse continue to feed, branches bobbing up and down under their weight. Yet the branches don't seem to break. *How do they do that?* I wonder, marveling at the balance required. And they each move to another tip to pluck their breakfast. *What a trick! They can bob and eat at the same time.* I begin to chuckle at the sight.

Then I think of what a trick it is for *us* to balance *our* lives—work, family, self-care, exercise. All of this besides maintaining some degree of relaxation, a social life, and having fun. And of course, there is the aspect of spiritual cultivation, too. It can feel as if we're a juggler in a circus — the circus of life. How do we balance it all without short-changing at least one aspect?

Our priorities seem to swing from one to another to another. But if one becomes dominant, requiring most of our time for too long, our overall health is bound to suffer—physically, emotionally, mentally, spiritually—it's going to happen.

Taking a break and reevaluating my priorities works for me, but it's hard to do, to *find the time* to do, *make* the time to do. But it is essential to *do* it.

Time for self? I always felt selfish when I tried to get time for *me*. Therefore, I could easily move that to the bottom of my list. Actually, it needed to be at an equal level with the rest.

At the end of the day, we need to ask ourselves one question.

Did I feed my body, my mind, and my soul today?

And we may not cover *all* our bases *every* day. There are surprises in life that can upend us. But even at those times, we need to integrate time for us—to step back and just *be*—even for a few moments, a few minutes, maybe for an hour. If we let one area of our life become the priority for too long, it will affect other areas, and our body will let us know.

It's the spiritual aspect that I neglect most easily. It seems I always have some task to do . . . but do I *need* to do it now? I am important, too; just as important. I know the feeling that I'm not as important has its roots in my childhood. That became blatantly evident as I delved into healing the childhood traumas I described in my first book. Yet I'm aware that the trauma still affects me somewhat, and I catch myself sensing a slight feeling of being inferior again. But it's rare now—an improvement, for sure.

Are *your* priorities in sync with your values?

Is your body telling you something?

17

Hidden Footsteps

~~~~~~

We received a foot of snow with the last Nor'easter. It landed on cold, barren soil, the rest having melted with the previous thaw. This is the first day since then that I've gotten to walk on my favorite trails; I'd been avoiding them earlier due to the depth of the newly fallen snow.

With the rise in temperature, the twelve inches of light, dry fluff has decreased noticeably—several inches. And with the sun shining on it, it has settled even more. So here I am, walking on my familiar paths instead of the plowed sand and gravel road I'd been using for several days.

I feel the tiniest brush of wind cross my face and whisper in my ear. I catch my breath at the crisp, coldness of it, yet it's not as cutting as in the depth of winter. There's a lightness to it—almost refreshing—as if it contains within it the promise of spring.

I stop. I sniff . . . and sniff again. Nothing—only the sharpness of cold in my nostrils. It's as if the air is giving off an *absence* of scent—withholding the mixture of springtime fragrances that awaken my being in late March or April. I awaken now to the beauty that can lie within starkness, too.

My gaze drops.

The first thing I notice in the snow is prints, each one showing three very long, narrow toes branching forward from a common center point where they all seemed joined. The prints line up one behind the other—five trails in all, side-by-side, each in a line. How I would have loved to see that—a flock of turkeys, strolling down our path, on their way to a feast of seeds somewhere.

As always, I'm here to see if Nature has anything to tell me—or just to enjoy time out of the house during these colder days.

As I wander on, I come to a protected part of the path where the interlocking canopy of softwoods shelters the trail. Here, hardly any snow has collected on the ground, though the lofty boughs are heavily laden.

The ground is still frozen here, the frost not willing to leave the comfort of the cold forest floor. As I trudge up the trail, there is a hollow sound as if I'm walking on a thin, firm crust over only air. *How can that be?*

Looking down at my feet, I see space—vacant areas surrounding rocks that had shifted with the thawing and freezing, leaving gaping holes in the ground. *That's why it sounds so hollow.* The freezing of the wet ground has caused it to expand and lift upwards, retaining its frozen hardness. I almost expect to break through at any moment, but it doesn't happen. I move along, safe and secure—the strength of thin, frozen ground.

As a member of a support group, I was once told that I had "some façade" by another member. I guess I was like the frozen elevated ground, presenting one image to the outside world of having everything together while the real person lived within, feeling empty and as hollow as the remaining spaces filled with air.

Are we afraid of what others might think if they knew the real us? I wonder.

Moving along again, I stop up ahead. The forest has opened up, and the path before me is white again and glistening in the sunlight. Diamond-like sparkles are everywhere—green and red and blue—shining and reflecting the light.

I see something in the snow. Footprints. *But how? I haven't walked here in days, certainly not since our recent snowfall.* Then it hits me. The footprints are mine, the last time I walked here. There were only a few inches of snow on the ground at that time. The prints had compressed the snow and now, even though they had been covered by many inches of *new* snow, they were again made visible by the melt. They had been hidden for days and were now uncovered.

It reminds me of my experience of discovering that my body had been hiding heavy metals in my tissues, especially tin and mercury, and they had reached a toxic level.

My doctor had suggested I take a provoking agent before drinking an amount of water. The agent causes a surge of heavy metals from the tissues. Getting a *normal* urine sample only tells us what's circulating in the blood at the moment. I wanted my history—what was being stored in my tissues. Something told me I *needed* to know that. I collected my urine over the next six hours. A sample of the combined urine was then sent to a special lab.

My mercury levels were off the charts—fifty-three, when the safe levels were less than four. My tin scores were fifty-four compared to the safe level of less than 10. Reading the lab print-out, I learned that a toxic level of mercury alone and even of tin alone can result in demyelination around the nerves, a cause of function loss in Multiple Sclerosis. I had both toxicities. *Could that be affecting my symptoms, too?*

But where had all this mercury come from that had collected in my tissues? I rarely ate fish, except tuna once in a while. I did have a large amount of dental work done during my junior-high years. Then the fillings were all amalgam, which contains a high level of mercury. During drilling, the mercury escapes into the air, and we breathe in that vapor. Compromised, cracked, or deteriorating fillings can also leak the mercury.

I also discovered that the township of Watson, New York, where I grew up, was a hot spot for mercury contamination due to the fact that industry in the Midwest was allowing it to be carried in the winds coming across to the East. Our water, soil, and air could have had a large amount of contamination.

There were also the balls of mercury that I played with as a child from a broken thermometer. It was fun to tap them with my finger and watch them roll, ever so easily.

Finally, I found out that mothers transfer heavy metals to the fetus as it grows in the womb. My mom could have had an amount of contamination that she passed on to me unknowingly.

With sensitivity to most medications, etc., I decided to detox slowly with tiny green tablets of chlorella, a single-celled algae that attracts heavy metals to it like a magnet and carries them out of the body as waste.

I have continued to eat salmon and tuna, but I am careful to get only line-caught, flash-frozen fish from the Pacific Ocean and never farmed fish. If my dentist is removing an amalgam filling, he is sure to have his assistant spray lots of water in the area where he is drilling. The mercury is then eliminated in the expectorant and not into the air as vapor to be inhaled. Over the years, I have had many fillings removed. Actually, there is at present only one left.

I can't change where I grew up or the mercury my mother's body may have contained or the contamination of the food I ate or water I drank or the air I breathed while growing up. But there are things I *can* do now—slowly remove the amalgam, use only composite when necessary to fill cavities, be selective about the fish I eat, live in an area with clean mountain air, drink only spring water from my drilled well—six hundred feet below the surface—and keep taking chlorella, a natural green that is healthy for my body and that continues the detox. At last note, my mercury level has dropped to the low teens, still not in the safe range of zero to four, but a far cry from fifty-three. My tin score is now in the safe range.

As I stand here on the snow-covered path, I see an analogy between the now exposed footprints ahead of me that had been hidden by eight inches of settled fresh snow and my body, which had been hiding the heavy metals stored within my tissues.

The footprints had been uncovered by the sun's melt of the new snow and my toxicity had been uncovered by symptoms that couldn't be ignored. The revealed footprints will melt away in time as my toxicity will continue to melt away also, with what I am trying to do to give my body the support it needs to accomplish the task.

The body always tries to rid itself of unwanted harmful substances that are taken in. But the mercury that I was taking in was to such a degree that the normal bodily procedure of ridding unwanted substances couldn't satisfy the amount being absorbed. Hence, it was stored in my tissues; hence, my body finally let me know that it needed help.

Thank you, Nature, for allowing me to better understand what's been happening in my body; it's so much clearer now. Thank you for the boost to my confidence that I am on the right path. Now I understand your message and I will continue to persist on my journey of detox.

Is there a message that Nature is trying to communicate to *you*? Is there something—a buried emotion, a scar, a hurt, a physical symptom—that's been covered up for too long?

Find a place to sit—on the ground, the sand, a rock, the grass. Sit in a chair with your feet bare and resting in the grass or in the sand or on the rock. Move your toes and feel the surface. Let Nature enter you. Absorb her. Feel the connection. Let time pass.

And may you *also* come to understand.

spring

Puffed and billowy, pink in hue,
  Lady Slippers huddled in the morning dew.

Quietly standing so straight and tall,
  Your message is clear, yet your stature—
  so small.

You show us the way, with your blossom so new,
  To survive in the forest of life—so true.

Some of you lean, some stand straight and tall
  Like a cluster of people, I seem to recall.

So why can't we see how we should live life—
  Trusting, blossoming, doing what's right.

Helping each other, no matter their state,
  Giving, receiving, it's never too late.

For humanity rings, with goodness and truth,
  And we need to give thanks for our learning
  and growth.

18

Spring Awakens

S pring has arrived. A smattering of snow lies heaped on the ground here and there, lingering still, resisting the meltdown. The ground softens as the fleeting ghost of winter exits on cue.

A flock of Canada geese, arranged in their familiar V-formation, honk their way in a southerly direction, marking their return from a northern hiatus.

Air temps are in the thirty to fifty degree Fahrenheit range now, almost daily. The snow is still crusting on the mountaintops, while drizzling rains are forecast for us down here in the valley.

A flock of flitting sparrows goes twittering by, erratically flying in and out and about one another.

A pair of graceful hawks soars in the cloudless sky. *I wonder if they're the same pair that was here last year, having returned to inhabit our valley after a long winter's absence.* I watch them catch the air currents and float effortlessly over the fields below.

Yes, spring has arrived.

I awaken to the sound of drumming, somewhere in the forest. It starts out slow and increases in speed, then quickly stops. The whole pattern is repeated. It's a ruffed grouse attempting to attract a mate—another sure sign of spring.

As a child, I would hear that sound, imagining someone was starting a motorcycle somewhere on our back road, never knowing the real source. As an adult, reading about the grouse was fascinating. Then I chanced to witness the chicken-like bird perched on a woodland log. It raised its wings to thump against itself rapidly, thus explaining the sound I had awakened to while growing up.

Now I am here on my property, awakening to that identical thumping sound. It makes me feel calmed as it penetrates my sleep, and I open my eyes, reminiscing about my childhood days.

Springtime rituals amaze me, and all creatures have them. As I walk down the driveway, something startles me.

I hear rustling to my right. All of a sudden, another ruffed grouse comes running out of a collection of young, leafless maple trees and runs across the driveway. It seems in quite a hurry. *It must be a male; his tail is fanned out—beautiful.* I can see the jet-black neck feathers are puffed out as he moves first one way and then another. He seems smaller than the females I've seen but is quite a handsome fellow. He also does a quick, twitchy movement with his head, every few steps. I watch, engrossed with the fanfare.

Since it's mid-April, with the nesting season around the corner, I'm probably not the only one attracted to this spectacle. Hopefully, he'll find a mate nearby.

A memory comes to mind, going back to one summer when we heard that familiar drumming all season long and wondered if there was a lonesome grouse out there, still looking for a mate. While walking in the woods, we found a pile of grouse feathers on the ground. We concluded his future mate had been served up to a hungry coyote on the hunt. The memory fades and I realize I can still see this parading grouse.

Besides his colorful display, he's probably claiming his territory, marking it out, staking his claim to this part of the forest. And I realize it's what we would call our home. This is going to be *his* home, a place to begin his family, and sorry will be another male that treads on his lands.

All creatures have territories. With some, they are simple and compact. With others, they can be quite vast, covering miles. And then there are the creatures that migrate.

We all need a place to call "home," a place of familiarity, a place of comfort. And for us, it can feel very special to return to that home. There are memories there, hopefully some positive ones. It's a place of belonging—roots, if you will.

Many times, there are negative memories of the past. And some people feel those memories need to remain there—in the past, not to be thought of again. But I have found, through my own experience, that reliving those past events and fully grieving them can be a step in healing from those experiences.

As creatures have homes or territories, territories have boundaries, as do we. One boundary is our personal space, and few people are allowed to enter that. The thought is, "Get out of my face." When really what we are saying is, "You're standing too close to me and it makes me uncomfortable." The other person has crossed a fine line and entered our personal physical boundary. And we all have them. Some people accept others into that space easily, once they are familiar with them. Others hesitate longer. And with some, we'll never be allowed in, and that's their choice.

Besides our physical boundary, we also have emotional boundaries. Some people seem to wear their emotions, and we can easily tell how they are feeling at that moment. Others present a façade. I was pretty good at that in my past, especially when I was out in public. Everything seemed to be a secret in my growing up years, and I tried to hide what was going on at home at all times. Now I feel more genuine, and it's a more relaxing way to live.

I've also noticed I need to "shut down" at times of deep emotional struggle. I might sit and just stare or lie down for a while. At these times, I don't want to see *anyone* or have a conversation. I'm preserving my core and need the time to "let things lie," to just *be,* allowing me the space to bring things to resolve. And I do.

I'm also aware of my psychological boundaries. When I was growing up, I couldn't seem to please my father, no matter what I accomplished. He was constantly criticizing me. So I began to construct a wall between us that acted as a protection of my core stability. And I knew he couldn't hurt me anymore. I shut him out, pulling a cloak around the person I really was. At the time, it was a form of survival.

After years of being made to feel less of a person, I reached a point where I couldn't cry anymore or hate myself anymore or think of myself as pitiful anymore. Yet I find it's still a reaction that begins to creep in, even as an adult. Old ways of feeling about oneself are hard to change.

Even as we build these emotional and psychological walls, we can dismantle them, too. It *is* possible. It requires a firm intention to do so. We begin to notice that we only begin to build the walls in certain circumstances with certain people. Even *that* we can change.

We can become more comfortable within our physical boundaries. I know that I can stand closer to people than I used to, and I'm more comfortable with that; my physical boundaries have lessened. Then again, I have seen people who present a very stiff persona. Yet when I try to give them a hug, they actually begin to relax and reciprocate. But it may take time—years of opportunity—to have numerous contacts. Familiarity plays a definite role, as does healing any negatives we hold against them.

Territory and boundaries—we all have them. It's fascinating to discover the purpose they serve and to notice if they have changed over time.

Take a walk outside or sit on the ground with your back against the trunk of a tree and let the wisdom of Nature help you identify your own personal boundaries—physical, emotional, and/or psychological—and how they affect your relationship with others and them with you.

Feel her presence . . . hear her voice.

19

Pellets of Ice and Icicles

stand outside, watching the ice pellets fall upon the light brown shingled roof of my home. They hit and bounce and bounce again, scattering in patterns as if they'd just been released from captivity.

The atmosphere temps are a mix. Hence, there are neither drops of rain nor flakes of snow. Just balls of ice.

Watching the scene before me makes me think about how I often feel as scattered as they, bouncing from one thing to another—sporadic and unsettled. It's that feeling of being bombarded.

Bombarded by what? I ask myself.

The answer comes—*by ideas, tasks, and commitments.*

It's difficult to have only one idea to come to rest, one thought to focus on, one idea to develop. I see myself in those scattering bouncing balls of ice as they strike the rooftop and scatter everywhere.

That's how I am when I feel overwhelmed; I yearn to escape *all* the ideas, *all* the tasks, *all* the commitments. At that point, I close down. I stop thinking, doing, and reacting. And I realize I need to gauge my tasks and commitments better and not take on so many. The state of overwhelm is not a pleasant place to be.

Maybe I sit down and work on developing one idea by writing a poem or essay or just journaling about my feelings at that moment. I can sit and listen to some relaxing music, maybe Nature sounds. I can do some watercolor painting or pencil sketching.

I need to let my thinking-planning mind close and allow my creative mind to take over for a spell, giving myself the break I need.

I have found that taking a walk in Nature and soaking up her peace and calm settles me. Ideally, I take my sketch pad or journal along—not on days when ice is falling from the sky, of course, but in better weather. Afterward, I'm calmer and clearer, and I can decide on the next idea to develop, the next task to perform and accomplish, the next commitment to fulfill.

Time passes as I stand there, watching and thinking. The thickly blackened clouds slowly creep across the sky. The ice pellets lessen in their onslaught, until they stop altogether.

The March sun peeks out, radiantly shining down. The air temperature begins to rise. I can feel the warmth on my face as the sun takes over its reign in the now clear sky, the darkened gray giving way to the deepened blue.

Turning to set out for my daily walk, my eyes catch the glisten of the sun's rays on a lone icicle, adorning the corner of the house. I remember as a child knocking icicles off the roof edge of my parent's house. It was almost as much fun as selecting one of them to suck on for a while, being careful not to get my tongue stuck to it. I learned the hard way, when that's exactly what happened the first time I tried to do it. Memories. . . .

As I focus on the icicle, the sun's warmth is having its effect; it begins to melt, melt, and drip and drip and drip. I've seen icicles melt numerous times over my lifetime, yet now I feel like something is also melting within me. Besides my relating to the feeling of being overwhelmed as I watched the bouncing balls of ice, I sense another message for me here.

Is it anger from the past that's melting inside me?

I know it takes *time* for an icicle to melt. It requires warmer temperatures and maybe the sun shining on it, even if temps aren't quite high enough. It also takes *time* for anger to melt and transition into understanding and acceptance. For me, it also takes love—love *of self*, love *from others* and love *from Mother Nature*—to begin the melting process. The more love and support I feel, the more the intensity of the anger lessens. And with loving support, the melting happens quicker.

Negative emotions dampen our spirit. They take away our light and plunge us into darkness—a darkness that falls like a shadow. It changes us into complaining, negative, and short-tempered people. And we've all experienced anger, justified or not.

I make it a habit to take my negative emotions to Nature and relax into her loving, non-judgmental support. I feel her warm breath on my face like a soft kiss, soothing and calming me; I listen to the sounds of melodious birdsong; I watch the light dancing on the vibrant green plants and stately trees. I touch the soft, cottony leaves of new sprouts emerging from the softwoods, and I look up at the sky and watch the puffy white clouds changing shape as they scurry by.

I spend time in her loving arms, and my anger recedes. She replaces the scars formed by the scorch of anger with the pearls of understanding and peace-filled hope.

And I know we're together on this journey we call life. I am not alone in my pain. I feel her presence everywhere I look. She is always there with me—always there.

~~~~~

Spend some time in Nature and allow her to cool the anger that now stifles you. It may be hidden, buried deep within. Tell her what you need. Feel her presence. She is there for you.

20

Metamorphosis

sit on a grassy bank at the edge of a long, narrow body of water. This grassy spot may be the only one to be found as I look out at the scene before me.

There isn't a beach here, just an opening in the scraggly trees that hug the rocky shore. Their branches reach far out over the water like arms, yearning to touch the last of the sun's rays before it sets on the far horizon. Some limbs appear battered and broken. They hang down toward the cold Adirondack waters, awaiting their final plunge. Few leaves are present on these dying gray fingers, which once sprouted the lush green buds of life.

The air is still; the water smooth and undisturbed by ripples. I hear the continual beeping of a nuthatch coming from the mature pine forest surrounding the lake. I picture it moving up and down the tree trunks looking for some tasty bugs to devour, while some chickadees join in with their twittering calls.

Movement on the left catches my eye. My focus shifts to a boulder resting there like a pinnacle in the still waters, lying askew in its position. I notice many rocks lie about as if thrown there without any plan. More movement. . . . *What is it?*

I move closer to see. It looks like an insect case splitting open, releasing its guest. The beetle-like form is metamorphosing . . . into . . . what? As I watch, it becomes more evident.

A dragonfly. I watch the entire process—*amazing!* I've never seen this before.

The new dragonfly wobbles in its stance on its new appendages, acclimating to its present and novel environment. It slightly moves its four wings, raising them ever so slowly into a horizontal position. Each wing will have the ability to move independently of the others, enabling it to fly forward or backward at will.

Ever since it was a larva in a tiny egg, this creature has lived in the water, growing within its exoskeleton until ready to metamorphose into a beautiful dragonfly. *And I was here to see it happen.*

Woe to the unwary mosquito, hovering above this narrow body of water, for it will be a much sought after prey for the predator dragonfly.

I once witnessed a monarch butterfly, emerging from its chrysalis, totally changed from its caterpillar stage. I watched in amazement as it clung there and then, with somewhat dry wings, took its maiden flight to a nearby tree branch to continue the drying process. It kept unfolding and folding its wings as if in a motion of fanning. And then it flew away—delicate and free. I felt as if I were flying with it, and my heart soared with the feeling of being freed from encapsulation.

As that memory begins to fade, I start to think about pollywogs. They also begin their life as eggs laid in water, this time on the water's surface in a jelly-like mass of round clear balls with a black speck inside. Looking into the mass, I've watched the tiny black dots grow bigger week by week, until they unfold and eat their way to freedom as a pollywog with a darkened tail and gills for breathing.

In time, the body grows fatter; the tail grows longer. And over the summer, four tiny legs begin to appear along its swelled sides. At the same time, the tail begins to recede. Eventually, the pollywog takes to land, having metamorphosed into a young frog, making both land and water its territory.

Many creatures go through metamorphoses. That happens to us, also. We begin as a fertilized egg and, in our liquid environment in the womb, grow into a fetus. We leave that liquid environment and are born, escaping our confinement. We take our first breath of air as babies and grow into children, then adolescents, then adults. At each stage we're changed from our original, sometimes making it nearly impossible to recognize who we are. Our features have changed as our bodies have grown.

Yet there's another metamorphoses that goes on *within* us, spurred onward by our encounters with life itself. We have been evolving into *an awareness* of who we really are. We move from dependence to independence. We begin to make our *own* way, establish our *own* values and our *own* priorities. At times, that may require us to move away from a relationship, as difficult as that may seem. We close one door and open another. We begin to recognize and seek out the atmosphere that will allow us to continue to evolve with the support we require. And in that atmosphere, our talents are honed; more gifts are discovered and allowed to be developed.

We begin to shine. Our own metamorphosis is occurring.

Have you closed the door on something in your life? What did you discover about yourself?

Nature is there for you wherever you are, wherever you go. Her calming presence can be your guide in making decisions and discovering who you really are. Trust in her guidance as you follow the path.

Nesting Site

ooking out my living room window one spring morning, movement catches my eye. There's something in the tall white spruce tree to the left of my view. It stands there as if in submission beside an ancient white pine with its delicate branches that look like so many green bottle brushes extending toward the sky. That pine must be a hundred years old if it's a day. The spruce, on the other hand, has branches that droop to the ground before the tips rise skyward.

Each species of tree seems to have its own pattern of growth, its own shape that it presents in the wildness of Nature. It's similar to races of people—each having a specific pigment of skin color, characteristic structure, and even gait. I never thought of that analogy before.

I catch movement again through the drooping spruce branches.

Removing the binoculars from the wooden stand beside me, I focus on the area that caught my eye. It's not always an easy feat to find that space in a tangle of crisscrossing branches with needles protruding everywhere. As I try to focus the binoculars, a tan-and-gray bird flies into my view with an object in its beak. It looks like a twig. Now I recognize the bird—an Eastern Mourning Dove.

The mournful sound of its call has awakened me for the past few days, once right outside my bedroom window. I move my binoculars around and notice another bird sitting very still on an inner limb of the daunting, fifty-foot tall spruce. I can make out its tail, a dark eye on the side of its head, and a beak as it perches parallel to my window.

"They're creating a nest right before my eyes," I whisper to myself. I'm thrilled.

As I continue to watch, the male keeps bringing twigs to the site. The female sits and reaches out over the edge of the pile and pulls the twig in, nestling in the collection of sticks. She continues forming and shaping the nest to her body, adjusting twigs as she sees fit, making it comfortable for herself and the two eggs she'll likely be laying. She'll need to keep the eggs warm in this nest of twigs until they hatch. It also needs to be strong enough to support the two hatchlings and future fledglings. I find it amazing how this collection of twigs can do either. Yet this is the way of mourning doves.

All of a sudden, both male and female fly to the ground and begin pecking on seeds dropped there last fall by the dying grasses, now exposed due to the snow melt. The foraging continues for maybe ten minutes before the female flies back to her nest and the male again searches for twigs, carrying them back to her. And on it goes until another break time to eat.

A subtle message sinks in. One I often need.

It's an important reminder to me of the need to take breaks in whatever tasks I may be about—a little recuperation time. Here the focus is on the final product—the nest—completed and strong and comfortable. And it takes time to build it that way.

I tend to perform a task nonstop until I'm finished, often exhausted and grouchy, driving myself needlessly to the finish. I can take a lesson from these mourning doves.

Before and after working, I watch the female and male perch side by side for a bit. He seems to be in a protection stance beside her as she sits on the somewhat formed nest.

As the days pass, I notice that work on the nest occurs only in the early morning hours. After that, the birds disappear for the rest of the day. *I wonder where they go . . .*

Suddenly, the familiar sound of the Pileated Woodpecker breaks in. I return my binoculars to their resting place and proceed to my back door, removing my teal quilted jacket from its metal hook. *Where is he drilling today?* I wonder. Opening the door, I get a better idea just where that is.

The tree he's attacking is nearby, actually at the end of our driveway. I can see the wood chips flying erratically as I approach, piling up at the base of an old gray stump about ten feet tall. The bright orange color of the chips again surprises me, as deeply hidden as they once were under the steel gray of the outer trunk.

I continue watching the bird, searching for the insects it uses for food, and I begin to think about the message here for me. *What am I searching for?*

I know it's sometimes hard to get to know certain people, hard to get through that outer bark they present to the world. And there are scars along the way for them to heal before we can get to the brightly colored inner core of their soul. We, too, have to pick out the bugs like the woodpeckers do, to expose the core. We need to look deeply to see the value that was there all along. This thinking leads me to the effect of first impressions.

I begin to ask myself if my first impressions are always accurate. Nature has shown me that I need to dig a little deeper if the impression isn't positive. I know the answer to my question. *No, first impressions are not always accurate.* Yet sometimes, that's all there is time for.

I really need to consider other things like body language, mood, interests, and concerns. I may need to share some of my own to try to find common ground. That would give me a more accurate impression of them.

If I take the time to look deep inside, I just may find a brightly colored core that's been hidden all along.

~~~~~

Listen . . . look . . . see . . . .

Dig deep within Nature and open your eyes to the beauty waiting to be discovered—by *you.*

Rainbow

t had been raining all night and most of the day, pounding on the roof and tapping at the windows. Now the sky was getting lighter, moving from a deep gray to a milder hue, and the rain was subsiding to a light patter.

Looking out my kitchen window, I stared at the horizon where the mountains stood soaking up the gently falling cloud-shed. All looked a verdant green; all looked refreshed. All was quiet—no pitter-patter of raindrops on the shingled roof as I heard last eve when I lay down to sleep.

The sun began to break from behind the bank of darkened clouds that had been pulled over it like a blanket. A smattering of latent thinning clouds moved across the sky, wiping away the darkness and exposing the blueness beneath. I felt mesmerized by the kaleidoscope of color constantly changing before me.

Since I love walking outside after a rain, I decided to get ready. It's a feeling of soaking up Nature's cleansing as if I were being cleansed, too.

I reached for my green rain jacket hanging by the door and carefully zipped it up, not wanting it to get stuck as the cloth lining puckered. I knew that the leaves on the paper birch and fluttering-leaved aspen trees outside would be heavily laden with the accumulated droplets as I sauntered on my way beneath them. So, even though the rain had all but stopped, I still needed protection, lest I become as sodden as the ground on which I walked.

I glanced out the window again and *there it was*—the faint beginnings of spectrum-color in the sky.

Outside, I watched as the rainbow continued to form. At first it seemed like a vertical shaft of faint color, the colors quickly becoming more definite—first, red on the far right side, then progressing to orange, to yellow, to green, to blue, to indigo, and finally to violet on the inside left of the shaft. This pillar of many colors lasted only a few moments before the bending began. It continued to curve across the sky, until the rainbow shone as a complete semicircle.

The colors seemed to blend into one another like butter melting in a pan, each reaching and comingling with its neighboring color. I couldn't tell where one color ceased and the next began. It was so complete as to hide any boundaries at all. Actually, there *were* no boundaries, just an exact and utterly complete blend at the point of joining.

I thought of what I experience when I'm embracing someone I love. If neither of us moves, I do not sense any boundaries at that time, either. I cannot tell where I leave off and the other begins. We are one for the moment of the embrace, so similar to my view of the colors in the rainbow.

As I stood there, the colors began to shimmer with a vivid brightness as the failing sun reflected on the remnant water droplets in the air. With the bow complete, the sky itself seemed to glow with a cantaloupe-colored hue, surrounding part of the bow. The other part of the bow was backed with the darkened grayness of the passing storm.

It was now 8 p.m. on May 4th. I stood watching in wonderment of it all. It was an experience of lightening and darkening of colors as they deepened with distinction.

As I stood there gazing at the spectacular ongoing scenario of colors before me, a second rainbow began to appear on the still-darkened part of the sky. It wasn't as bright as the first—much more muted—but followed the same configuration. And the colors, not the shape, were reversed in their order of softer presentation. The inner color of the arc on the second bow was red, like the outer color on the first bow. Then there was orange, yellow, green, blue, indigo, and finally violet. As I watched, the colors in the arc gradually widened, dissipating and fading away.

I'd never thought much about rainbows before, but this time the experience blossomed with meaning.

Nature had bathed me in the beauty of the rainbow, which does not form in a clear sky; it requires darkened clouds and rain—lots of rain. Only after the appearance of the sun do we then see the beauty of the rainbow being created. The process is not prolonged; it is fleeting. It does not last. We must catch it by being in the right place at the right time. The occurrence is not a guarantee and does not happen with every rainstorm.

After a struggle or even *while* I am struggling in my life, I must remember that within the struggle lies the promise of a rainbow. An opportunity will appear to guide me to the bow—to a solution, to a remedy. But it may be fleeting. And will *I* be in the right place at the right time, unencumbered by anger or envy or jealousy or bitterness? Will I catch it or will I miss it entirely?

I need to keep myself in a healthy state of body, mind, and spirit to deal with what life sends my way. I need to look for the rainbows in my life.

～～～

Spend some time in Nature and allow her to increase your awareness, helping you to now recall the rainbows in your life, past and present. *Focus on the rainbows.*

Turning the Soil

~~~~~~

When spring arrives, I look forward to one of my favorite experiences—gardening. Whether it's vegetables, herbs, or flowers, the garden calls.

Lifting my metal, wooden-handled trowel from the canvas pouch where I keep it, I start out for my much-loved piece of earth. I've never been one to wear gloves when gardening, much preferring to dig in the soil with bare hands. Though my dry and stained fingers are testimony to where I've spent my time, I savor the feeling of moving the earth with my hands. I see it truly as gift. Whether fine sand or more granular soil, it's a kinesthetic thrill.

I place my trowel into the dirt and watch it go deep, particles of soil falling to the sides as it pushes down . . . and down . . . and down. . . . My goal is transplanting some unwanted growth from this area of my garden.

I remember my mom removing "weeds" from among her flowers when I was a little girl. She was not gentle with them at all. It was like they were the enemy and needed to be destroyed. My philosophy is different. To me, weeds are just misplaced wildflowers. They need to be removed and transported to another resting place to root. I feel no antagonism against them. As far as I'm concerned, they're just in the wrong place at the wrong time. And maybe they are preventing my select flowers from flourishing.

I enjoy having wildflower gardens of blue flag, black-eyed Susans, and wild daisies, with purple vetch leaning and twining their delicate tendrils around the stem of a neighboring plant.

Simplicity is there. Design is there. And they are beautiful in their own right, with myriad colors and characteristics entirely different from every other plant species. Some are spikey and tall like common mullein, while others creep along the ground like moss flocks. Some like shade, such as the lily of the valley; others prefer sunshine, such as wild daisies. And some are very versatile in their habitat, such as those black-eyed Susans.

The fragrance of wildflowers can be as sweet as the delicate pink milkweed blossom or as astringent as the striking yellow blooms of the dandelion.

The shape, size, and number of petals astounds me when I think about it. And all the different hues—just amazing. I am reminded of an artist's palette, but in this case, Nature is the painter. Her careful hand is at work.

Vegetable gardens are for a different purpose; that is production. The planting of vegetable and herb gardens is usually to yield some food or flavoring of food for the planter and/or the wild animals that may frequent the area. The artist's hand is at work here, also.

The soft tendril vines of snow peas abound with green pods that hang vertically to the ground, contrasting with the large-leafed bush string beans—both yellow and green varieties. The oversized leaves of the zucchini and yellow squash contrast with the thin yet numerous and much smaller bracken leaves of the tomato plant. And then there are the long, tapered leaves of yellow sweet corn, whose tall stalks reach up to the sky, contrasting with the shorter and multiple stems sprouting from the kohlrabi plant.

Some plants display their yield above ground, as the above-mentioned examples, while others shoot out tubers below ground, such as the sweet potato. Some plants grow edible roots, including the crunchy, elongated carrot and the sweet-tasting and rounded red beet.

Whether above ground or below, we look forward to the harvest providing nutritious, home-grown, organic food—the best Nature has to offer.

Nature calls forth our creativity, whether we're at work among the flowers or planting vegetables for food. And many artists are inspired by the shades and shapes and lighting that Nature provides. Whether the paints on their palettes are oils or pastels, watercolors or acrylics, artists are enamored by shape, shade, and light, carefully attempting to emulate what Nature demonstrates without thought and with abandon.

Many poets seek the outdoors, not only as the setting for their creation, but also for their spark of inspiration. And writers are painting pictures, also, using words to brush-in the scene for the reader, be it a physical setting, an emotion, a thought, or an idea.

Nature has inspired my own creativity. Having dabbled in watercolors for a time, I was amazed at the vast number of shades of a specific color. With sketching, the concept of negative space was startling to me. I learned about composition, line, and perspective, with Nature as my guide. And my writing and poetry has Nature at the forefront. Where would I be without her?

~~~~~~

When was the last time you let yourself "go" and experienced Nature's silence and beauty?

The next time you see a field of wildflowers, take some moments to admire Nature's handiwork. Notice the creative masterpiece of color, line, and light. Allow her to unleash your own element of creativity, whether it is in working with wood, metal, cloth, clay, food, or words. It may be hidden deep within you, waiting to break the surface. Allow Nature to take you to that point, to help you develop the creative gifts that are already there, implanted within you.

It's All in the Timing

~~~~~

The day dawns gray and gloomy with a darkened overcast of cloud cover. The snows of winter have all but melted away, except for a pile here and there where the plow sought to push a mound of it, an enormous mound of it. That still remains—chunks of ice unending. It will be there for quite a while, maybe even throughout the spring.

Everywhere, as I look through the forest of hardwoods, I see gray and brown. Last fall's dead autumn leaves lie scattered, cast off in disarray amid the brown of the pine needles, having blown in after being shed as the cold temperatures of late fall descended.

I'm anxious for spring to come. I'm *always* anxious for spring to come after a long and frigid winter. Spring awakens something within me; I feel more alive and energized. I feel like I'm expanding, opening up and releasing tremendous amounts of energy that has been tucked away all winter.

The wildflower buds lie in wait; tips of hardwoods are only slightly colored; softwood sprouts of soft green needles are still on hold. It's as if they're testing out the still-cool temps before making their full debut. Yellows, pinks, purples all stand like dancers just behind a green curtain, waiting for the stronger sun to cue their entry.

I'm on hold, too, wondering if we'll still get another snowfall. It's happened before. At this time of year, it can be quite discouraging when it happens. Yet there was excitement in the air at the very first snowfall of winter back in November. Beginnings are *usually* more exciting than endings. It's the timing of *when,* in the winter season, the snow falls—at the beginning or at the end.

Among the first wildflowers to appear in the spring are the delicate pink lady slippers, also called moccasin flowers because of their puffy and billowy shape. Growing on our bank, under the very prominent green canopy of the hemlock trees, they huddle together, giving support to one another—kind of like a family of people. They all have the same purpose—survival. And don't we? With their pretty pink coloring, they make me smile when I see them. They bring joy to me, the viewer of the velvety soft blooms. Though some of them are budded, they hesitate to open. It's not time yet.

And I focus on people, thinking, *Isn't it the same with us?*

For some people, it takes an enormous amount of time—many years—a time of wait, of hesitation before they burst into bloom. It's all in the timing, and no two of us are alike. It seems we're each on a different clock and, like in the fairy tale *Cinderella*, we're awaiting our pumpkin coach to take us to the ball. Someday our time will come.

Throughout our life we have disappointments, frustrations, and discouragements, and yet, when we least expect it, our pumpkin coach arrives and opportunity presents itself. Our "coach" may take the form of a person, an idea, an activity, or a challenge. Some of us spring into action, quickly seeing the opportunity for what it is. Others sit back and wait and think about it all, reasoning it out to see if, indeed, it really *is* an opportunity to respond to with action.

So, do I move to a new location *now*? Do I apply for that job *now* or do I *wait* until it's offered again, *if* it's offered again? Do I trade my car *now* or do I *wait*, do *more* research, and reconsider once the new ones are out?

We make our decision, and we only know, in retrospect, if it was the best thing for us to do at that time. Or do we?

Do we ever really know for sure, beyond a doubt? Sometimes we do. Many opportunities come to us as we live our lives. Sometimes we jump and other times we decide to wait. It truly is all in the timing.

I've noticed that a harsh word spoken today, when the listener may be feeling downtrodden, can cut to the core and have a devastating response within, giving the feeling, at the very least, of being hurt, if not saddened and depressed. Yet when the same spoken word is expressed next week, and the recipient is feeling confident and somewhat jovial, the response will probably be totally different. It may be dismissed entirely, as though the speaker is just having a bad day, with no offense being taken at all. Or it might be taken as a point made and worthy of future thought, but not the least devastating.

When we're feeling good, when we're in balance—body, mind, and spirit—we react to life's happenings with greater resilience. Yet, being human, our reserves of energy dip at times, and we can wither under harsh treatment.

I've noticed that besides the particular *word* that is used, the *tone of voice* used to express the word can affect how the meaning is interpreted. The same word spoken harshly can destroy a person, while that same word spoken kindly or jokingly can bring thoughtful repose and spur the possibility of growth.

Life is made up of a multitude of choices—*Do I do it? Do I do it now or wait?* Only I *can* answer. Only I *will* answer.

Our intuitions—those feelings that reside in our gut—are our connection to the Universe, our "voice" if you will. That "voice" within can lead us in ways that fulfill our connections so that we may, indeed, follow our own unique path.

I spend some time in Nature thinking, *am I connected? Am I on my path?* Only *I* can know when the bud within me awakens, opens, and bursts into bloom.

And it will—perhaps today. Or very soon.

I wait with excitement.

Breathe in the breath of Nature and allow her to help you to choose what's best for you *right now.* Is she leading you to something new, or is she telling you to be patient and wait? Is spring coming quickly, or quite slowly? Is your "coach" arriving, or must you wait and walk slowly to the ball?

Feel her support of your choice. With eyes open, watch, observe, and interpret her message. She is there for you.

summer

Resting on a bracken wall,

So tight and so secure,

Clinging as with all your might

With colors bright and pure.

And there you stand for all to view

Yet nary do we see

That you are regal in your stance,

So proud are you to be.

And you persist, with beauty rare,

To stand there in the mist,

On foggy days—like you, so rare—

Your presence, we have missed.

Reflection

~~~~~~

t had been raining all night. I could tell because of the large puddles on the driveway when I woke. Shedding my pajamas, I pulled on my denim jeans and blue T-shirt. I felt comfortable in blue and wore the color often. Blue reminded me of blue skies and morning glories—two sights that cheer me instantly. I grabbed my raincoat from its hook and ran out the door, barefoot.

I ran over to the nearest puddle and splashed right through, then on to another and another—jumping, running, splashing. Water flew everywhere as I let fly all my cares and worries. I felt like a kid again, and was glad I gave in to that desire.

Rain puddles are magnets for children. *Why is that? I wondered. Does it remind them of the womb they left behind*

so recently? Is it natural to want to feel immersed in water?
Feel it on their skin?

When I tired of splashing, I moved over to a nearby puddle and stood at the edge as the ripples subsided. I noticed the patterns in the sand, formed by the movement of water, that were caused by my early morning jaunt. The area surrounding the puddles was now dotted with black spots, drying in the sun that had peeked out. As its rays struck the puddles, a steamy fog began to rise vertically from each one. I watched, mesmerized by the scene. It was like each puddle was smoking as the water vaporized and rose, curling into the air.

As the fog cleared and the sun continued to warm the puddles, in sharp contrast to the cold rain that had previously fallen, the steaming puddles became lakes of sparkling diamonds—glistening, shining, and flickering specks of light as they reflected back to the sun its own light.

As I looked deeper into the puddle I was standing near, I became aware of another reflection. This time it wasn't of the water but of a person—me. It was so clear. No wind stirred my image. I could make out my face, my hair, even my blue T-shirt, which had been tucked beneath my raincoat. My raincoat had been blown open by my puddle-running escapade, which now also had exposed my jeans.

But what else was there for me to see? Something about the water caught my attention. Or rather, something *on* the water.

A light breeze stirred the surface of the puddle, and as I watched, my image became blurry. So much so that it seemed to disappear all at once. It began to reappear as the breeze softened. It was as if I were looking in a two-way mirror. I began to wonder, *Am I more my true self when I am balanced, exhibiting patience and a sense of humor? Then I'm more accepting of myself and others.*

When I lose focus, as in my blurred image in the puddle, do I become unbalanced as my negative emotions take over? Like I'm a different person—critical, complaining, envious, jealous?

Anger, frustration, and fear have that effect on me. I seem to bring out the negative in others then, also. They become hurt, defensive, or scared. They cry, yell, or withdraw into themselves. My demeanor causes others to reflect back to me a similar state. Is that why arguments go on and on until one or the other either resigns herself to keep peace no matter how she really feels (people pleaser) or asserts herself, stating how she truthfully feels?

A faraway memory invades my mind.

When I was teaching, I remember overhearing hurtful,

degrading comments being made about a particular child by one of my coworkers.

"He's just like his brother. Cut from the same mold. And look at his parents—no wonder . . ."

The child was in kindergarten, just having turned five that summer. I had him in physical education class and had no problem with the child. But did I speak up and express my own experiences with the child? Unfortunately—no. I held in my own irritation and frustration at the comment.

How often I have avoided unpleasant situations instead of speaking the truth, kindly but firmly. I do not know how my truth will ultimately be received, but at least I can be at peace having voiced, in this case, my own experience with the child.

We were two different people with two different experiences and, therefore, two different opinions—nothing more. By not expressing my truth, the interpretation could be that I am in agreement with the speaker even when I'm not. I'm just keeping the peace to avoid confrontation. I have become a peace keeper not a peace maker.

It is hard for me to believe that *any* child is totally bad—a tortured soul, maybe, but not totally bad. He or she may have poor behavior patterns, but that is where we come in and work to change the behaviors that have given the child such a poor reputation.

If we assume the worst, we will get the worst. If we look for the worst, we will find the worst. Think of this the next time you experience conflict in conversation.

~~~~~~

Ask yourself, "Am I the peace keeper or the peace maker? In this situation, which do I want to be?"

Remember, kindly yet firmly, speak your truth. Now ... is your reflection blurry ... or crystal clear?

A Spring-fed Lake

'd just gotten back from a short hike and I couldn't wait to cool off. I was sweating profusely, as the air temperature was in the nineties. I knew of a spring-fed lake on the way home.

That should do the trick, I thought.

Pulling my car into the small parking area at the edge of the road, I grabbed some dry clothes from my back seat and took a well-beaten, quarter-mile, woodland path down to the lake. When I broke from tree line, there it was. The lake looked like a many-faceted diamond encased in a setting of green. It looked so inviting. I could hardly wait to feel the pristine waters envelop my skin with that refreshing coldness that enlivens blood vessels and also my spirit.

After changing out of my sweaty shorts and T-shirt into clean ones, I left my sneaks and walked barefoot to the water's edge. Feeling the sand oozing between my toes made me chuckle. I love walking barefoot on sand—the tickling sensation always makes me smile.

I came here often when I got really hot; it was pretty and it was private. No one else was around. Sometimes I came here to sketch or to write. I found the solitude inspiring and consoling.

The day was sunny. Blue skies surrounded the puffy white clouds. As I looked around, I could smell the scent of pine and hear some ducks quacking in a nearby bay. A gentle wind blew warmth across my face.

Time to get wet.

Stepping into a spring-fed lake in the Adirondack Mountains is always a chilling experience no matter what the air temperature reads. The first sensation was of frigid water since the source was a combination of springs, bringing water from hundreds of feet below the surface, and fresh water streams that also fed the lake. The streams funneled water from this past winter's snowmelt, some of it draining from the Adirondack High Peaks region. Even knowing that ahead of time, it still took my breath away. There was no pre-preparation possible to prepare me for that initial sensation.

At times, the water's edge seemed a bit warmer, especially if the air temperatures had been in the seventies and eighties for a few weeks. But that hadn't been the case this time.

Standing at the edge of the lake, I tried to prepare myself for how the chilling water would affect me. I took a deep breath and held it as I edged my toes to the water.

I'm in!

The small wake created by a passing canoe lapped on the shore and heaved the water to my ankles. I gasped as the sensation hit me as if my feet had suddenly been encased in ice. I jumped backwards. As the wave disintegrated, I again crept to the water's edge.

I'm so hot—I've got to cool off.

I've always been a person who gets wet slowly, not like some who prefer to run and dive in all at once. Does that have anything to do with the fact that I don't like taking risks? I like to have some assurance—some idea of what I'm getting myself into, even though that may be an illusion.

Okay—walk. Move forward one step at a time.

And I realized that whatever challenge I face, if I

proceed in a forward direction, one step at a time, it isn't so bad. It isn't so overwhelming. I just need to break my challenge into parts. And that's what I did, moving step by step . . . deeper and deeper . . . until I was immersed in that cold and refreshing lake water.

Delightful!

This process brought to the fore a memory—that of being diagnosed with Multiple Sclerosis.

The first thing I did back then was to gather information about the disease. And then read . . . read . . . read.

I attended a workshop on stress to understand more about how it can negatively affect our health. It made a lot of sense. Then I began identifying the sources of negative stress in my life. Some I could accept, and some I wasn't ready to accept. After that, I made the effort to begin to eliminate them, one at a time.

I began to give my body support through supplements, and finally made some definite lifestyle changes. I was helping myself and moving forward. I wasn't sinking in a quagmire of mud, stuck and floundering.

I still don't run and dive into lake water, but neither do I stand at the edge and then retreat. My method is to go slowly, one step at a time, to accomplish my goal—and that's okay.

~~~

What's a challenge that you're facing?

Remember, after deciding on the first step, take it. Trust that the others will become clear—and follow the path.

Refreshment lies just ahead, if you keep going.

27

Rotting Stump

Walking along the quarter-mile dirt driveway from my home, my bare feet move along the dry sand. It's warm and soft and giving as my feet sink deeply into the looseness of it. The sand squeezes between my toes and slips off as I move.

The day is overcast with a low, gray cloud ceiling, and the weather report indicated the possibility of rain today. We'll see. As I move along, an old tree stump next to the woods catches my eye.

I've glanced at it before but never looked at it closely. For some reason, curiosity draws me today, and my steps turn in that direction. I move up a slight incline to where it rests, feeling something pulling me closer.

The stump sits in the center of an open space of drying grasses. Though there are healthy green trees in the surrounding forest, the stump is gray, with shreds of bark hanging from it, being discarded as so much garbage, littering the ground. As I get closer, I realize this is not just a rotting stump. A multitude of life forms sprouts from it, and I ask myself, *How could I have ignored this magnificent wonder for so long? There's so much to see here.*

A rotting stump in disarray
Yet filled with life in its final days.

Mosses and fungi clustered there,
Green-leafed vestiges with yellowing hair.

One lone pine tree settles in
Between dead leaves and rot so thin.

And a maple tree tries hard to thrive
Behind the pine—it seems to hide.

Atop this stump in vibrant light,
A spider ambles across the site.

Its eight long legs in full display
Amidst the moss green of its stage.

A sultry slug goes creeping by
Upon its velvet cushion it lies.

A mushroom livens up the scene—
Brown dots on white and round, it seems.

Grasses grow among dead bark
That's brown and black, starving and stark.

A pine cone here, a pine cone there,
All dry and shriveled—with nary a care.

Lichens spread downward on a bark base,
While old pine needles dress up the face

Of this old stump—so staunch yet serene,
Here in the woods like a reigning queen.

As I stand looking at this rotting stump, I wonder, *What do I feel is over for me in my life?* I know I will never teach school again and I know I will never climb mountain peaks above 4,000 feet again. But I sure enjoyed doing both earlier in my life.

Now, at age seventy, I realize I haven't lost the ability to teach, but it's not in a school. It's through my writing—showing others what I have learned through my experiences, especially in Nature. And the mountains I climb are much lower in elevation, but I enjoy them still and notice much more than I did when I was trying to climb as quickly as possible. Nature is wonderful, and I realize that more each day.

Out of loss can come a deeper appreciation, or we can let regret eat away at us. I guess I could sit around and complain and become depressed. That would probably stress my relationships within my family and cause them to distance themselves from me. Is that what I want? Would that make them or me happy? I don't think so.

I needed either to find something to replace what I lost or be able to accept modifying the particular activity. Since I can't climb the High Peaks of the Adirondacks anymore, I find the little nuances that Nature contains that speed had caused me to miss. On lower mountains I have seen the mass of delicate spider webs in the grasses and the hammered-out woodpecker holes in the trees. I've even found a yellow-bellied sapsucker nest and watched a parent feeding its young. I've been able to notice different bird calls that were drowned out by my panting breath before, and I've been able to follow and identify the bird calling. There are so many wonderful things in Nature to observe and discover and wonder about.

And though I no longer have a classroom, I realized a while ago that I am still a teacher—to my grandsons, to individuals wanting to know more about healthy living, to individuals inquiring about Multiple Sclerosis, with which I had been diagnosed years earlier. Only the setting in which I teach has changed.

A new perspective on things can be born out of regret and failure. I can begin to accept that I am not perfect. I am human. And as I accept that about myself, I find I am more accepting of others. Having been a perfectionist, that was a challenging discovery and difficult to swallow. I was embarrassed that I had developed a chronic illness when I was an example of what healthy living was all about. I felt guilty, as if I had intentionally caused this disease, when, really, it was healthy living in Nature that has been the example for others, showing them an alternative practice to self-pity and self-victimization.

Then a new realization takes over.

I have sometimes categorized old people as feeble and inadequate. As a young adult, I was uncomfortable around old people. Then I met and became close friends with a woman in her late seventies who was alert, intelligent, and worked full time, counseling burned-out priests and nuns. The wisdom that woman shared with me was beyond compare. Not only did she offer me her friendship; she helped me to begin to understand myself—believe in myself.

"Follow your heart and you will never go wrong," were the words I remember to this day. And they have proven true many times in my life.

It is not uncommon to ignore the elderly, especially as they encounter movement and posture challenges along with the breakdown of bodily functions. It is not uncommon to ignore their opinions, their voice. But I have been blessed with the wisdom of an elder and absorbed her experiences, and I feel honored to have been in her presence.

We all lose abilities as we age, but we can still honor and respect *every* age of our lives and realize we still have a purpose and usefulness.

In a field near my home rests an old stump, still providing life and nutrition to many, helping them to grow and be healthy. Just so, the wisdom of the elderly can enrich our lives, helping *us* to grow, too.

Listen to *their* voice . . . and learn.

Clouds

~~~~~~

close the door of my silver Ford Focus and place my feet on the dirt of the parking area. I stand, taking in the sight. It's high summer and the birch and maple forest spreads out before me, rich and green and filled with dense foliage. I notice what looks like lilac bushes at the far end of the parking area. Large elephant-eared rhubarb leaves cluster nearby, giving the area a hint of nostalgia as if it was once host to a cabin of sorts. Here in the Adirondack Mountains, lilacs and rhubarb are sure signs of past human inhabitation of the area.

No sign of any ruins from here, but I wonder what I would find if I got closer....

I gather my beach towel, small red cooler, and water bottle and begin moving toward the trail leading to the lake.

It's a beautiful day, I think. I can feel the warmth of the sun's rays as they meet my skin. They seem to linger there—soaking in, warming my whole body. I glance up, taking in the brilliant blue of the sky. My step is light, and I'm floating on air.

It won't take long to get there today, I think.

As I enter the forest, I hear the urgent cry of a blue jay announcing my presence. Joining in is the incessant chattering of a red squirrel high up in a sugar maple tree.

"It's okay. It's only me," I call.

They quiet, as if appeased by my voice. All is now still in the forest as I make my way to the beach.

I'm expecting the beach to be empty except for a couple of fishermen who routinely test their hand at catching a few trout. As I reach the beach, my eyes survey the scene. As I expected, the fishermen are climbing into their boat.

"Good luck today!" I yell. They answer with a friendly wave of a hand.

The mountains rise tall on the horizon and appear lower in height as they get closer to the edge of the lake. Cedars hug the shore, their lower branches trimmed by deer during the past winter. Evergreens are everywhere—pine, spruce, hemlock—crowding one another for space and sunlight.

The water level has risen since the rain last weekend, draining much of the water from the surrounding mountains. I see that the beach area has shrunk. As I look around, I see that there is still room for my towel beside the large outcropping of rock at the water's edge. I begin to spread it out, straightening every wrinkle. I place my sneakers, cooler, and water bottle on each of the four corners to anchor it lest a gust of wind upend it. With all of that set, I lie down on my back.

I relax into the sand, feeling a connection to Mother Earth. This is one of my favorite places to be. I close my eyes, listening to the gentle lapping of the water on the shore.

I try to quiet my mind from thoughts of all the tasks I could be doing right now while I take some time for respite. *I need this,* I tell myself. Still, thoughts of my sister invade my mind. There she is, eighty-five and living alone. I have to believe that her children are doing the best for her. *I wonder what my elder years will be like . . .*

I begin to relax every muscle in my body, beginning at my feet and slowly moving toward my head. I feel my feet flop out as the tension releases there. Slowly I move to my knees . . . then thighs . . . then hips. I continue up the trunk of my body to my chest. Next I concentrate on my fingers, allowing my hands to lie limp . . . then forearms and biceps. I hold most of my tension in my neck and shoulders, so I remain there longer as I allow the release. It seems to come in stages, peeling away like the layers of an onion. When I'm satisfied, I proceed to my jaw, letting it drop. I focus on my forehead, which is crinkled with concentration. Then I feel the tension escape out the crown of my head. I am nearly asleep now and in a state of just being.

As I lie there, a gust of wind sprinkles sand upon my face, tickling some, stinging a little. I lift my arm and brush it away.

As I open my eyes, I take in the sky above me. I can see puffy white cumulus clouds floating by. They look so unhurried, so free like puffs of cotton on their way to who knows where. As I watch, I see them take on the shape of a bird. Eventually, I can make out the shape of a dog, maybe even a tree. The clouds continue to change shape as they dance about the sky—gathering, separating, and passing one over the other. Even the coloring changes from pure white to some areas darkening to gray. They retain their puffiness and when the wind picks up, they respond accordingly, racing across the expanse of blue, taking the disappearing animals with them.

I think how I sometimes float through life and at other times I race, feeling driven to achieve—what? and why? When I'm floating, I am without stress. I feel no pressure. I have no deadlines. When I'm racing, I feel driven, sometimes with the intention of reaching a goal and sometimes to some ending I can't even see. And I wish not only to reach that goal or ending but to get there quickly and efficiently. *But what is my goal?* I wonder. Talk about pressure.

Being balanced is somewhere in between.

Where are *you* right now?

If you're racing, feeling ungrounded and flighty, try stepping outside wherever you may be and take a moment to look up at the sky. What do you see? Is it clear? Are there clouds?

Even if you are not where you can see the open sky, breathe deeply and let yourself "float with the clouds" for a bit. Then come back to earth and go about your day.

If you are feeling floaty, you may need to ground your-self. Try sitting on the ground with your back against the trunk of a tree and focus on the roots reaching deeper into the ground. If trees are absent, sit upon the ground, close your eyes, and imagine yourself resting against a tree. Feel the trunk at your back and lean into the tree. Feel the tree's strength enter you. Absorb it. It is there for you.

When I'm balanced, I exude a patient and loving kindness, radiating love. I care about and honor myself and others. I can give and I can receive and be accepting of others' differences. To be in balance is to be in a state of health.

~~~

Allow Nature to nurture you and modify the extremes. Allow her to enter you and feel her love.

The Peeling White Birch

stand at the edge of my lawn. The white birch shines brilliantly in the morning sun. At forty feet tall, this starkly white tree with black horizontal striations and blemishes amazes me. The striations seem as little stripes scattered throughout the bark. Older limbs have broken off in places, leaving blackened knots where a living limb once grew. This gives the tree a distinguished look and makes it easily identifiable.

The verdant green leaves dot the branches in great contrast to the white of the barked trunk. Fresh spring shoots of young, heart-shaped leaves extend out from each branch's tips, projecting the new growth outward from this living tree.

The bark itself is peeling outward, serving as evidence of the expansion of the trunk as it grows. Pieces of shed bark lie scattered at its base. The scene reminds me of how *my* skin less dramatically sloughs and a new layer forms underneath, pink and healthy.

Picking up a piece of shed bark, I place it in the palm of my hand and examine it more closely. I carefully peel back some of what appears to be the top layer of the bark. I discover that the piece is made up of multiple very thin, tissue paper-like layers, reminding me of phyllo dough. And they are surprisingly fragile, breaking apart in my hand as I try to separate them from one another. Yet the multiple layers bring strength to the protective covering of the tree.

I begin to think about people and what multiple layers of love and support do for us. In my personal experience, the more people I know who love and support me, the stronger and more confident I become. As my confidence builds, the more secure and safe I feel. I can better handle any negative critical comments without dissolving into a sea of depression or erupting with a volcano of anger. I am able to calmly consider the negative comments and either accept or reject them—no grudges held.

Then there is the inner strength we develop through *our* offerings of love to others. It's like we're giving back without thought. And it doesn't have to be the same people who gave to *us*. Love is the connection, and it empowers us and emboldens us.

As I look at the piece of shed bark in my hands, I notice that though the outer layer is a pure white, the reverse side of that outer layer is a deep red, with white striations. As I again remove layer after layer, the red deepens even further. Again, I feel a strong appreciation for the fragility of life, yet how strong are the combination of the fragile layers.

On the trunk itself, the new bark underneath, where the shed piece came off, is pink, again like our new skin. These similarities amaze me.

So, what do *we* need to shed so we can grow? Hurts . . . and fears? I've healed some hurts and conquered some fears. And then there's guilt.

Guilt eats away at so many of us. It tears us up inside and blocks our goodness. It can go on for years, compounding its effect on our health. We may want to punish ourselves for the words we spoke, the act we performed. We'd do *anything* to undo it. In hindsight, we know we'd never do or say that again. If only we'd known the situation *then*, or what the outcome was going to be *then*. But we didn't.

Forgiveness of self is a tough row to hoe, but a necessary one if we are to unveil hidden gifts within us and free ourselves to become more who we really are.

Blaming ourselves seems to be an automatic response, but it doesn't help us. Admitting our part in the misdeed and accepting *some* responsibility may help if it, in fact, is true. We need to ask ourselves these questions: What was my intention? Did I lack all the facts? Was I aware of what the outcome could be? Was I informed as to the options? What baggage was I carrying at the time? What baggage were *they* carrying at the time? These are the same things we need to consider when someone else has hurt *us*. Why not ask *ourselves* the same questions?

At these times, I find that taking my plight to Nature has resulted in a workable idea that has alleviated the emotion. I go for a walk and feel her support and guidance. An idea arrives; wisdom enters; direction comes. And then I know my next step toward releasing my feelings of guilt.

I look again at the peeled layers in my hand and my thoughts drift to the layers of healing that our bodies go through. I am still shedding heavy metals and going through "healing crises" or cleansing. The more toxins I have to dispel, the more serious the crisis. Some of my old symptoms return, which was scary at first. I thought I was beginning another flare-up. Then I realized that these were my *old* symptoms. A possible flare would be indicated by *new* symptoms.

As my healing progressed, I would periodically plateau and then take a few steps backward, while my body purged itself of more toxins at a faster rate than could be properly disposed of. When that happened, I would cut back my commitments, rest more, and spend more time in Nature. It might take days, weeks, or months, but I would come through and be at a higher level of functioning than before my crisis. At first my "healing crisis" seemed to appear every four months, then every six months, then once a year, and then every few years. I know my body is always trying to heal itself, and some crises I probably don't even notice. But the big ones I can now identify. And I give thanks! I am so grateful that my body has a way of ridding itself of heavy metals, encouraged by my taking chlorella. It also tries to rid me of harmful bacteria, parasites, and candida through healing crises. My body is eliminating all the waste products through all elimination channels and setting the stage for healing. And yours is, also. It just needs us to give it the support it requires.

I think of healing as coming slowly, step by step, building health—layer upon layer like the bark on the white birch. The combination of all the layers will make us stronger and healthier. Whether it's an emotional, psychological, or physical healing, it usually takes time, with setbacks along the way. Invite Nature to walk with you and within you—and heal.

Remember, the rainbow comes *after* the rain. Look for the rainbows in your life. There are many.

~~~~~~

Sit outside in the air. Feel the breeze tickle your cheek. Allow Nature to help you recall all those people in your life who provide that loving, supportive base you require to discover who you really are.

And give thanks. You have made a very important connection.

Feather

~~~~~

On my walk today through a hardwood and evergreen mixed wood, a feather appears in the path ahead of me. In the dappled sunlight falling through the canopy of leaves, I squat, lift it gently, and let it rest in the palm of one hand.

This one is large, with brown and white markings—a turkey feather, probably from a female.

I am always surprised by the feathers I find. I have never gone looking for them. They just seem to appear before me, and I treat each one as a surprise gift. As a message I must read.

To think that feathers like the one I am now holding insulate and protect the bird from any inclement weather amazes me. I say that because I have accrued some tail feathers from males already, and they have iridescent tips that shimmer when I move them in the light.

This one is striped—brown and white—not dark and shimmering.

There are many different kinds of feathers on a turkey, with multiple designs of color. What does this brown-and-white striped feather say to me? Brown is the combination of yellow and green. Yellow is a color of healing and positivity. Don't I feel better on a bright day splashed with golden sunlight? Green calms me and speaks to me of new growth like what comes in the spring. So I interpret the message of this gift-feather this way: I will become aware of new positive growth within myself in the near future.

The feather feels smooth and silky to the touch. As I stroke it from quill to tip, I notice how intricately woven the feather is—what protection from cold and moisture it can provide.

Turkeys, like all birds, spend a lot of time preening their feathers. Automatically, I do the same thing as I stroke the feather, lending my natural oils to that of the feather. I feel a connection to the earth as I handle it.

What occurs to me about turkeys is that I usually notice them in groups, strutting together, even roosting with one another in trees at night. Inherent in them is the energy of sharing. Don't I feel some of that energy when I share of myself with others, too? Is this feather reminding me of the benefits of sharing myself with others and not keeping to myself so much?

> Silken threads
> Entwined together—
> Insulating, protecting,
> In all kinds of weather.
>
> Blending, connecting,
> Colorful or drab,
> Plump full of meaning
> With purpose each has.
>
> Large bird, small bird,
> Raptors of prey,
> Tiny little creatures
> Bringing tidings that may
>
> Cheer you or sadden you,
> Depending the day,
> Feathers all together,
> Having their say.

Some other thoughts begin to enter my mind.

Birds molt periodically and drop their feathers, much the way animals shed their fur. With some animals it's due to a seasonal change, during which they trade the thinner, cooler coat of fur for a thicker and warmer coat for the winter months.

We humans also shed our head hair. Normally, every four months, one-third of it gradually releases, and new hair begins to grow. We may not even notice it, but as with all animals, something may trigger a greater-than-normal loss at any one time. Here, stress and trauma play an important role. For humans—loss of a job or a loved one, an accident, a miscarriage, an illness—anything that qualifies as a loss to an individual may qualify as a cause. Hormonal changes or a lower functioning thyroid are other possible triggers. My thoughts begin to take me back to another time. . . .

My comb seems to be filled with hair each morning. I've been noticing that after I take a shower, hair has collected in the drain.

This was the case after my mother passed away. I loved her, but we were never really close. I was the baby of the family and was born after a previous miscarriage. I don't believe she ever really bonded with her new little one. I felt estranged from her all my life, as if I were somehow born at the wrong time. It wasn't until I was in my middle sixties that I began to understand why.

So why was my body dealing this way with so much loss of hair? I knew I was grieving her passing, but this seemed so much more . . .

Maybe it was *because* I never felt close to her, felt her love for me, felt her approval, heard her compliments. Maybe that's why I was reacting this way. This was traumatic for me not only because she was my mom but also because I felt I never had a *real* Mother. I'd always wanted one who would laugh with me and cry with me; someone I could share feelings with, such as fear, anger, and love. My body was telling me that one day I would have much to heal concerning the relationship with my mom, but not right now. Now I was to grieve. . . . My mind slowly returns to the present.

For birds, new feathers grow in as the old ones are shed. For humans, a newness of life can result once hurts are healed. It isn't easy to heal hurts, but it's worth it. It took time and energy to identify the underlying causes of the distance between my mom and me.

Hurts are carried in our cells long after we stop being consciously aware of them. Gradually, they can have a negative effect on our health. That is, until we face them, recognize the situation, and take the necessary steps to heal the hurt within our mind and body.

Do you still carry the hurt caused by a past event or a relationship that needs healing? Is now the time?

Carry your hurt to Nature. Accept her support of your pain and allow her to absorb it. Listen as she lends insight and understanding of it. She does not judge. Enjoy her gift of solitude and listen to her sounds.

She is there to listen.

She is there to help you heal.

Birches Entwined

stand on the pine needle-covered path and gaze off into the mixed pine and hardwood forest. The first thing I notice as I stand there is no sound. All is silent, even though I am surrounded by the forest.

Why? I wonder. No birdsong, no tree frogs calling, no insects buzzing. Only stillness. Even the air seems not to be moving.

Yet I can *see* life everywhere; it's going on without sound. The hardwoods are budding with bright red and yellow tips on the end of their branches; the softwoods are sprouting, dressed with a vibrant green at their branch ends, decidedly different from the rest of the tree. Fiddleheads poke through the Adirondack duff with a seeming enthusiasm for the season, while wild violets display their delicate royal purple blooms with pride.

I can *smell* life—the fragrances of the budding trees and wildflower blossoms, stronger now with accumulated moisture from last night's rain. I hold my breath to allow the combined scents to radiate within me and reach deeply into my soul. I feel light. I feel free.

The forest floor is damp from the rain, and I'm picking up a scent. It's the scent of rain-soaked earth—heavy, humid, moisture-laden—and I feel like I'm being pushed down by unknown forces, forcing me to squat in this wild wood. And so I do. The heavy air makes it a bit more difficult for me to breathe, and I pause to take slow deep breaths. The scent permeates my being, and though it's more difficult to breathe, I feel invigorated by this entire experience.

I touch the wet leaves of a nearby young sugar maple, hardly five feet tall, growing beside the path. They feel smooth and soft and wet. I pick up soil from the earth and close my fingers around my find. I open my hand, exposing the coarse bits of sand and small stones and debris—rotting leaves and twigs cast off by the rainstorm. I close my hand around my treasure and roll my fingers back and forth over the lot.

The sand and stones feel gritty and lumpy, but the leaves and twigs feel softer and defined—the shape and texture being the deciding qualities by which I can identify them. All of this is evidence of the ongoing life in the forest. And somehow, I can *feel* life there.

Streams of run-off begin to gurgle as they collect extra moisture and direct it elsewhere. A soft breeze touches me, flowing over my face, and above and around me the aspen leaves are stirred to produce their characteristic rustle. Now I can *hear* life, too.

The sound is wonderful.

Seeing, smelling, touching, hearing—that defines life in the forest. If I were more educated in the edible wild foods, such as mushrooms and wild cucumber, I could add taste to my definition of life here.

I look to my left, and my gaze halts as I notice two birch trees growing very close together. Their trunks are about the same circumference around. These twin yellow birches are standing beside another tree, a paper birch, which is older, as evidenced by its thicker, knotted white trunk. The yellow birches are more slender, have smoother trunks, and are decidedly shorter. My gaze lingers as I notice, for the first time, that all three trees are not only standing close together but seem to be entwined—branches crossing and crisscrossing, intermingling and touching. Even the trunks of the two younger birches are twisted around each other.

It seems the trees are reaching out, lending support to one another as they grow. And in so doing, they lean into one another and buffet the exceedingly strong winds that sometimes go gusting through, threatening to uproot them from their anchored spot.

All three share the same glowing sunshine that enhances food production in their leaves. Their roots share the same soil from which they each absorb the same nutrients needed to sustain and nourish them. And the droplets of rain provide the moisture necessary—the satisfying drink of life.

I've witnessed before young birches entwined with the parent tree beside them, supporting and clasping the parent as if in a hug. This time, as I stand there with my appreciative gaze on the trio, I am reminded of how good, how emboldening a sincere hug can be. It uplifts us and communicates a feeling of safety and security. It seems to recognize and ensure the goodness present in each of us. It is a joining, a melding of two people in a bond of caring—a bond of love.

The three trees demonstrate a direct analogy to people and our need for social contact and support. We need to know there is someone we can lean on if we need them, be it a parent, a sibling, a friend, or a spouse. The need may never arise, but it's good to know we can count on them to help us out.

In the forest, I have seen trees of the same species entwined and also trees of different species entwined in the same way. I think of different races of people and how we intermingle and lend our support, too. Nature shows me that it doesn't matter—same or different—they are all trees and we are all people.

As a child, I absorbed an attitude that people from different races, different nationalities, and different classes were not welcome in our home. We were of the lower economic class and, therefore, mingled only with the same. And yet, looking at the forest, I see many species of trees and many species of other members of the plant kingdom all growing there. I see a thriving community of varied species all living together.

The blend is beautiful.

~~~~~

Spend some time in Nature, recalling a time when you needed to lean on someone and just knowing that you could call on that person made you feel more secure. You knew he/she would be there for you if you ever needed.

Are you willing to be another's leaning-post?

Epilogue

~~~~~~~~

t's early morning. The sun is breaking on the far horizon. I open the front door of my tiny home and step outside, inhaling a deep breath of fresh, invigorating air. Moving a few more steps to my forest knoll, I gaze at the white pines standing as sentinels to the rest of the forest. One in particular towers above all the rest, as if it's proud of its longevity. And that's as it should be in the scheme of things. Old age is to be admired.

This past year, I turned seventy and became a member of what some may call the "old age" category. *So,* I ask myself, *what have I learned at this point in my life?*

I look out at the vista before me and know that I have learned that Nature is strong and wise and healing. I find support and comfort here, within her arms. But there is fragileness about her, also; she can easily be taken for granted and abused. She is not a permanent structure for us to take from and reap the benefits. She is here to share *with* us her wisdom and healing—emotional, physical, psychological, and spiritual. It is through her example that we learn. Without her, we cease to become.

As I stand here in the early morning fog, I feel a light, cool mist kiss my cheek, and I smile. I do cherish these moments. Standing here, I view the majestic mountains before me and the pristine valley below. A gurgling stream wanders through the glacier-carved gorge, watering the myriad hardwoods and softwoods on the hill above. The entanglement of brush and ferns drink thirstily as they cluster on the bank, while the ever-alert deer and rabbits feed on the plants and tree leaves nearby.

The water in the stream flows into a distant placid lake where some will evaporate. The resulting clouds will gather and cause rain to fall, again watering the hardwoods and softwoods on the hill and the brush and ferns on the bank.

Living plants are able to make their own food through the effect of sunlight on chlorophyll in their leaves. Through absorbing the carbon dioxide released by us and other animals as we breathe and the presence of water, oxygen is released—oxygen that is necessary for our survival and that of all the members of the animal kingdom. Besides supplying the very gas we need to breathe, plants become *our* very food—a symbiotic relationship for sure.

Connections. Everywhere, connections. . . .

We say we have human nature, but do we really understand that? We are only beginning to understand the intelligence and language among other animals. All forms of life have energy and communicate; they just use different mediums, if you will—sounds, vibrations, waves of energy—at levels we may not be able to detect. *We* are the illiterate ones where they are concerned.

We may think of ourselves as supreme beings on this planet, but that is only what we tell ourselves because we are able to think and have a verbal language we understand. Yet we are discovering that even plants communicate in a way *we* cannot hear or oftentimes make meaning of. But we are learning—learning we are *different,* but not necessarily superior.

Because of our minds, we can think and make choices and are responsible for the result of the choices we make. When we come to realize how inconsequential we are in the scheme of things and accept our role as a unique, yet equal, and vital part of the very fabric of life, only then can we achieve an authentic state of peace. Once we feel the connections with our heart *and* our mind, we will know our mission in life is to live *with* the Natural World, appreciating, respecting, and preserving that gift which surrounds us at all times.

We are simply the human *aspect* of Nature—one tiny thread in the spider's web—the web of life. With all the threads joined together, the web is connected and strong, enduring and of purpose—a cohesive whole. If one thread weakens, it weakens the whole. If one thread breaks, the web is eventually destroyed in its essence. It will be forever changed. It will never regrow. It will hang limp and loose, floating about with the gentle breeze, serving no purpose, none at all. We need every thread of the spider's web in order to survive in a balanced and healthy way. Otherwise, we will cease to become.

The field of reflexology teaches us that places on our feet and palms are connected to our specific organs and organ systems. By providing pressure on specific points, we can release blockages and cause a dispelling of toxins. Circulation improves, and we feel better.

We can use the energy from rock crystals and the energy present in essential oils from the plant kingdom to help lessen discomforts in our muscles and joints. We know that our muscles are connected to our bones; ligaments connect one bone to another. Tendons play their part, and we move. We move through connections within us and with Mother Earth.

The process of entrainment in our brain when we hear birdsong as we wander in the woods allows the alpha brain waves produced to give us a feeling of calm and relaxation. And what about the soothing *flavor* of peppermint or the sweet *smell* of lilacs? I find those also produce a feeling of calm.

Nothing is an entity in and of itself. And we are a part of it all.

Movement to my left catches my eye. I turn, noticing the sun's rays glancing off a glistening, dew-wet spider's web, dancing in the soft breeze. It extends from the twisted branch of the staghorn sumac tree to the thorny stem of a wild rose bush. The threads holding the web are attached to various twigs, thorns, and branches. As I gaze at the web, I feel an opening of my heart, an opening of my mind, an opening of my soul.

And I get it. I know my soul purpose. I see the connections in the Natural World and realize I am an important part of that—I am a vital thread of the spider's web.

Each thread of the intricate web represents a part of the Natural World, and each is connected to the other. No one is more important. No one dominates. We are all equal, bound to each other by a common thread—the same life force—and it dwells within every form of life, yet is greater than all of us. Each part of the Natural World is a different presentation of that same life force, each as important as the other.

And with that awareness, I begin to realize that I have a *responsibility* to help maintain this Natural World.

With that awareness at the forefront of my mind, I begin to turn down the wooded path, thinking of my own personal journey. The path seems to be bending to the right. I hesitate, stop, and glance back over my shoulder. I see how far I've come—in experiences I have had, choices I have made, and wisdom I have gained.

A smile dances across my lips.

I turn and face forward around the bend—awaiting new experiences, new choices to make, and more wisdom to absorb.

And I know I am not alone on my journey, *never* alone. Nature is *with* me and *within* me. She is *beside* me and *leading* me onward. I can feel the pull now in my soul.

Which dances

with

joy.

A Note of Thanks

To David Hazard, my writing and publishing coach, for all the encouragement and support you continually extend to this author. Your efforts are greatly appreciated, as are your editorial suggestions.

To Peter Gloege and LOOK Design Studio for your unique ideas and presentations that serve to greatly complement the text.

To Karen Price, my proofreader. Your eyes catch everything.

To my readers (Elaine Baker; Jay Federman, MD; Ralph Gordon; Bronwyn Seal; Natalie Smith; Dan Sullivan; Suzanne Weinrich) for your support and suggestions that truly serve to enhance my work.

To Gary, my best friend and soulmate, whose continuous support serves as a base from which I can create and formulate my words as I progress on my personal journey.

To my family and friends, always, for ongoing support and encouragement with my writing.

To Nature, of course, who has given me the strength and endurance to share her story with the wisdom of her words. You are always there, and I thank you for that.

About the Author

~~~~~~

Debby Havas lives in the Adirondack Mountains of northern New York State. There, she cares for her land and the plants and animals that live on it. She has chosen to live and work in small, rural communities her entire life.

As an educator, she holds permanent teaching certificates in physical education, health, elementary education, and family and consumer science, besides a Master of Science degree. In addition, she has raised two daughters who were and are her delight.

In her retirement years, she has devoted time to watercolors, sketching, and now writing. As author of two previous books, *My Journey to Wholeness* and *A Gentle Path of Healing,* she now completes her third book, *Connections,* as she seeks to continue honoring Nature as both her Great Teacher and Companion on the journey of life.

Made in the USA
Middletown, DE
25 August 2019